# Old Gentlemen's Convention

## The Washington Peace Conference of 1861

*Robert Gray Gunderson*

# Old Gentlemen's Convention

## The Washington Peace Conference of 1861

THE UNIVERSITY OF WISCONSIN PRESS

*Madison,* 1961

The basic problem of American history revolves around the question how a people diverse in origins and background, engaged in multiple economic activities, and occupying a vast territory without geographical unity could have remained a single nation. The answer is found in the American genius for compromise, for adjustment, and for conciliation. Compromise was the American way of life, and the spirit of tolerance and mutual agreement infused American religious beliefs, economic structure, and political apparatus. A century ago Americans recalled with pride that their Constitution was the product of compromises worked out in the Philadelphia Convention, they were familiar with the great compromises upon the Missouri Question in 1820 and the tariff and nullification controversy in 1833. In 1851 they were emotionally prepared to accept the complex body of adjustments known as the "Compromise of 1850" and to sign abnegations proclaiming the compromise a "finality."

Yet within the decade of the 1850's the honored spirit of tolerance and adjustment seemed to fade from American life. Intense economic rivalries, desperate political controversies, and a highly emotional crusade against slavery as a mortal sin brought a decline in interest in adjustment, a growing belief that the problems of the nation must be resolved by an absolute settlement. This nation could not long endure, asserted Abraham Lincoln, half slave and half free. It must become all one thing or all the other. Such arbitrary alternatives—ignoring the long endurance of myriad "Half-Way Covenants"—became the commonplace of political rhetoric. In Kansas Territory men rationalized shedding one another's blood by rigid assertions of unbending principles; in Congress, as a new animus possessed the lawmakers, men came armed on the floor and hurled invectives and challenges across the aisles; in public discussion men of press and pulpit assumed unqualified postures. In 1860, the Democratic party, splitting into unyielding factions, sacrificed unity and the hope of defeating the equally doctrinaire sectional party whom they labeled "Black Republicans." When Lincoln won a majority of the electoral votes, intransigent leaders took South Carolina and the Gulf states out of the Union.

Yet even as extremists of North and South were rallying behind uncompromising standards, voices of moderation, echoing pleas for traditional American toleration, tried to win a hearing for compromise. In 1860, a Constitutional Union party, resting its case on "The Constitution, the Union, and the Laws," assembled in convention and nominated moderate men—John Bell of Tennessee and Edward Everett of Massachusetts—for President and Vice-President. "There are many distinguished men on the floor," reported one skeptical observer, "but they are mostly 'venerable men' who have come down to us from a former generation of politicians." The convention delegates pledged themselves "to maintain, protect, and defend, separately and unitedly, those great principles of public liberty and national safety, against all enemies, at home and abroad, believing that thereby peace may once more be restored to the country... and the government again placed in that condition of justice, fraternity and equality... under the example and constitution of our fathers...." In the election in November, Bell and Everett polled a substantial popular vote and carried three states of the Upper South. To moderates, who added Stephen A. Douglas' votes to those of the Constitutional Unionists, it appeared that a majority of Southerners opposed the extremist Democratic party which had supported John C. Breckinridge, while Lincoln's Republicans did not have the approval of a Northern majority. It seemed, indeed, that the people of the United States might yet be led back to the American principle of compromise.

Although South Carolina and the Gulf states, under the leadership of extremists, promptly seceded, Unionists hoped for compromise. In Congress, committees of House and Senate considered a score of proposals looking to an adjustment of the question of extending slavery into the territories, returning fugitive slaves, and even for giving the South a controlling voice on all matters dealing with slavery and territorial expansion. Yet it was evident that extreme, or "fire-eating," Southerners and intense Republicans were more interested in throwing the onus of failure upon their rivals than they were in healing the nation's wounds. As hope faded for a Congressional settlement, Unionists turned their thoughts to a national convention.

The border state of Virginia sent out the call for a peace conference. Twenty-one states responded, and on February 4, their delegates gathered in Washington's Willard's Hall. The convention was, indeed, the last hope of preventing a divided nation and a civil war. It was, like the Constitutional Union gathering of the 1860 campaign, an "Old Gentlemen's Convention," and the majority of its members were committed to the traditive methods of political adjustment. There were, of course, radicals among them, but the fire-eating Southerners were not there. On the day that the old gentlemen assembled in Willard's, representatives of the seceded states met in Montgomery to launch the Confederate States of America. In the Washington Peace Conference men of good will prevailed over the extremists and sought for a formula that could unite the people against both the rabid Black Republicans and the Montgomery secessionists.

Professor Gunderson has studied the problems of the Peace Conference and carefully evaluated its achievements. In the fervid oratory of partisans, the doom of the conference was predicted from the beginning. Yet in the convention itself the members believed that discussion, negotiation, and human reason might produce solutions. The problem, as Professor Gunderson clearly sees, was a question of rhetoric: the old gentlemen needed to dramatize their position, to capture the emotions and channel the reactions of America's moderate majority.

Opponents of peaceful adjustment—the extremists from both sides of the Ohio—had reason to fear that the old gentlemen might accomplish their purpose. The conferees, as Professor Gunderson points out, had more than a modicum of success. They stilled the radicals in their own number, and they agreed upon compromise proposals which could have resolved the current issues. It was not the conference that failed. Congress failed. The minority party of the nation controlled the Congress and rejected the plan of adjustment offered by ex-President John Tyler and his associates in Willard's Hall. The moderate majority controlled neither the machinery of the federal government nor the apparatus of the political parties. They could not implement their appeal to reason, and the controlling minority rejected all suggestions for a referendum on the issues.

Professor Gunderson's study suggests important questions both about the American Civil War and about the machinery of democracy in times of crisis. Would a less rigid system of government in America have given time for new consideration of the changing issues, and have allowed the traditional methods of compromise to prevail? Could moderation be dramatized—in 1861 or in the twentieth century—so that it could overcome the partisan rhetoric which admits only unqualified alternatives to human problems? "The fatalistic sense of inevitability—the concept of the irrepressible conflict—in itself hastened the day of mobilization," concludes Gunderson. The conclusion may have pertinence even in another century.

WILLIAM B. HESSELTINE

*University of Wisconsin*

B efore most wars, representatives of contending sides meet in solemn, secret conference in an attempt to achieve a peaceful adjustment, a ritual designed ostensibly to apply reason rather than force in resolving questions at issue. In additon to this expressed purpose, such conferences serve several useful strategic functions, providing time to make necessary psychological and military preparations: to mobilize men and public opinion, to demonstrate the impossibility of negotiating with the enemy, to place the onus of war on him, and to reconcile indifferent citizens to war's inconvenience. In many respects, the Washington Peace Conference of February, 1861, was such a gathering. At the request of the Virginia General Assembly, 132 representatives of twenty-one states met at Willard's Hall in Washington, D.C., to find a solution to the crisis which eventually led to civil war.

Extremists, of course, had nothing to compromise; thus, all contenders were not represented. RADICALS in Wisconsin, Minnesota, and Michigan refused to negotiate with "traitors." SECESSIONISTS in the cotton states claimed that the day for discussion had passed and sent representatives to Montgomery to organize the Confederacy. CONDITIONAL UNIONISTS came demanding guarantees which would give Southerners reason to remain under the federal government, hoping that perhaps a satisfactory compromise might reconstruct it. UNIONISTS desired assurances of various sorts, but were ready to accept much less than their more militant allies; thus those who took stronger positions damned them as "submissionists," while they retaliated by ridiculing their detractors as "fire-eaters." Both north and south of the Ohio, those who favored conciliation were called moderates or conservatives, convenient terms for describing the combination of Unionists and Conditional Unionists, as well as for procompromise Republicans and Northern Democrats. Each contemporary had a highly personal meaning for the key word, *compromise,* an unfortunate semantic fact of political life then and an annoying problem, if not to say a source of disagreement, now.

This account is intended to supplement rather than to digest Lucius E. Chittenden's *A Report of the Debates and Proceedings*...(New York, 1864). It describes from primary sources the political, economic, and psychological setting of the Conference with an analysis of its audience, speakers, issues, and results. It presents material from unpublished diaries, memoirs, and letters in order to reveal motivations which may have prompted the words and deeds of participants. It assumes that persuasion influences behavior and rejects the doctrine of irrepressible conflict, a fatalistic concept which places political events beyond human control.

Footnotes and bibliography reveal a substantial debt to other scholars, and to librarians who offered experienced assistance in locating manuscripts, newspapers, and photographs in forty-five libraries in twenty states and the District of Columbia. Descendants of delegates obligingly re-examined their attics in a search for relevant contemporary documents. The editor of *The Journal of Southern History* permitted republication of "The Washington Peace Conference of 1861: Selection of Delegates." Virginia S. Gunderson typed the manuscript, shared in the research, and helped to eliminate errors in style and judgment. J. Jeffery Auer gave support and encouragement. Oberlin College granted the author a sabbatical during which he completed a part of his research. His longtime teacher, William B. Hesseltine, provided inspiration as well as the Foreword.

R. G. G.

*Bloomington, Indiana*
*September, 1960*

# Table of Contents

# List of Illustrations

*following page 66*

The Peace Convention, Willard's Hotel
Exterior of Willard's Hotel

*Delegates to the Convention*
Former President John Tyler
John C. Wright
George S. Boutwell
Salmon P. Chase
James Guthrie
James A. Seddon
Thomas Ewing, Sr.
Charles A. Wickliffe
William C. Rives

Zachariah Chandler's "Blood-Letting" Letter

Old Gentlemen's Convention

The Washington Peace Conference of 1861

## Chapter One

# A Day of Important Events

At dawn in the nation's capital on February 4, 1861, a stirring drumbeat roused "a host of night-capped heads" unaccustomed to the cacophony of reveille as executed on E Street by Company K of the Second Artillery, just recently arrived to forestall what radical Republicans described as a powerful Southern conspiracy to seize the government. Though seven states had passed formal ordinances of secession, moderate leaders still hoped somehow to hold together the raveling ties of union. As a gesture of assurance "more effective than the most eloquent speech," Senator William H. Seward of New York urged a prominent display of the Stars and Stripes; and with some embarrassment members of the Washington City Council approved an appropriation of $150 for a flag and flagstaff for City Hall.[1] A somewhat more alert functionary had already raised the symbol of national unity atop the yet unfinished Washington Monument, 228 feet above the ground. Contributions to complete this memorial to the Father of a dividing country continued to trickle in from the seceded states; and Georgia, though out of the Union, still advertised its state lottery—prizes from $5,000 to $25,000—in Washington papers.[2]

Awakening to what many felt to be a "season of riot and assassination," jittery citizens braced themselves for "a day of important events." Though hovering around the freezing point, the weather was not cold enough to provide firm footing in the muddy streets, and indifferent city authorities failed to keep gutters open and crossings clean. In many localities, according to the *Evening Star,* "the carcasses of dead animals" remained exposed and rotting for weeks. Not a sewer "blessed the town," as one disillusioned western Republican discovered; and the general agent for Dr. Montarde's MIRACULOUS PAIN KILLER issued a warning against the alarming prevalence of cholera morbus, diarrhea, and cholic, promising a "certain and effectual remedy."[3]

With the stock market continuing to sag, local merchants advertised panic prices, but lively diversions offered a welcome escape from dismal reality. The alert manager of the Washington Theatre on Eleventh Street, one block south of Pennsylvania Avenue, conducted his diversionary operation "with infinite enterprise and spirit in the face of the dull times." E. A. Sothern was billed as Lord Dundreary in the comedy, "Our American Cousin at Home," with no advance in prices: orchestra, one dollar; dress circle, fifty cents. Advertising one of the "most elegant and agreeable establishments" in the land, Gautier, the French restaurateur, invited epicures to test the superiority of his house. Gautier's rival who specialized in sea food asserted quite irrelevantly, "If you want to save the Union, call at Harvey's." Strangers suffering mishap with one or another of the city's five-hundred acknowledged Cyprians were advised to seek out DR. BROTHERS at 179 South B Street, where the very best medical and surgical treatment could be had "without fear of exposure."[4]

Across the street at the Smithsonian Institute, the more intellectually inclined could attend the evening lecture of Z. Wells Williams, Esq., on "The Literature and Government of Japan." A fair was opening in Thorn's Building for the benefit of Providence Chapel, and a concert at the First Baptist Church on Tenth Street featured the Amphion Quartette Club, the Partello Family, and the Choir of St. Paul's English Lutheran Church. That weekend, churches were well attended, with "numerous visiting strangers" enlarging congregations in the central part of the city.[5]

Across the Potomac, Virginians were balloting for delegates to a state convention, and editors speculated about a Unionist or secessionist victory. Contentious argument raged between those who wished to take the Old Dominion out of the Union and those who sincerely hoped for an adjustment which might permit them to remain with honor. Confronted with a disrupted Union, Northern politicians debated the necessity for making concessions in order to hold the border states. Northern Democrats staunchly advocated the compromise propositions of Senator John J. Crittenden of Kentucky, the basic provision of which re-established the Missouri Compromise line prohibiting slavery north of 36° 30'. Republicans were divided between conservatives, who endorsed concessions such as that of Congressman Charles Francis Adams of Massachusetts which would admit New Mexico, leaving the question of slavery to be determined by the people of the state, and radicals, who invoked the Chicago platform, urged federal officials to enforce the laws and punish traitors, and hoped for the passage of a force bill in Congress.[6]

Tempers ran high. One Massachusetts radical thought Caleb Cushing, a leading Bay State Democrat, "should be hung before the capital punishment law is changed." The Vermont delegates to the Republican Convention reassembled during the first week in February to oppose all concession as "a surrender of principle, which would effectually demoralize and destroy the Republican party." Extreme abolitionists joined William Lloyd Garrison in proclaiming, "The Union is assuredly going to pieces! 'Glory to God! Amen!' "[7]

Various economic motivations gave emotional intensity to constitutional and ideological rationalizations. Southern planters and business men cancelled or threatened to cancel orders to Northern firms; some even repudiated their debts. Alarmed at this collapse of Southern trade, Northern merchants re-examined their faith in Republican doctrine and urged Congress to make whatever concession might be necessary to prevent commercial anarchy. "Let party be forgotten if needs be," said one rueful capitalist, "to preserve the whole union."[8]

Office-seeking Republicans, on the other hand, had no intention of being deprived of the usual rewards of political victory. Industrialists hopefully anticipated passage of the Morrill Tariff pending in Congress. Land speculators, real estate operators, and railroad promoters pushed for a Pacific railroad and argued over its proposed route. Yeoman farmers looked acquisitively westward to the homesteads promised in the Republican platform. Caught up in the excitement, Washington women were "turning politicians," crowding Congressional galleries, and adding to the hubbub in public parlors. At the Capitol, Senators John Slidell and Judah P. Benjamin of Louisiana were scheduled to deliver valedictory addresses.[9]

Dispatches from two unusual political gatherings, however, raised more editorial dust than the fulmination on Capitol Hill. In Montgomery, Alabama, 830 miles to the southwest, three hard days and nights of travel at best, representatives of six of the seven seceded states assembled to form a Confederacy. Texas had passed its ordinance of secession four days earlier, and promised to be present forthwith; but the course of the eight additional slave states was still in doubt. Amid their immediate preoccupation with establishing a new government, Confederate leaders conjured with the perhaps even more important problem of precipitating secession in the Upper South. Above all, if only for prestige, they needed Virginia.

But representatives of the Old Dominion were gathering at Willard's Dancing Hall for a widely heralded Peace Conference called by its General Assembly "in an earnest effort" to adjust "unhappy controversies" and to afford the people of "slaveholding States adequate guarantees for the security of their rights."[10] That both bodies assembled on Monday, February 4, was not entirely coincidental—the one to establish a new government, the other to hold together the old. Commissioners from eleven states were already on hand in Washington, and still more were en route, though bitter legislative battles over the dispatch of delegates continued in several Northern states. The previous afternoon, a special Baltimore and Ohio train had brought many Western members, and the Willard brothers' hostelry at the corner of Pennsylvania Avenue and Fourteenth Street housed a majority of them. "Probably," speculated the editor of the *Evening Star,* "there were never before collected at one time together under a single roof so many men of note."[11]

Commissioners soon sensed the atmosphere of apprehension which pervaded Washington. Impressed by the "display of men and guns and cannon," those from the hinterlands compared the city to a warlike encampment.[12] In welcoming the Vermont delegation, Senator Solomon Foot talked excitedly of Southern "roughs and adventurers" and suggested the advisability of carrying arms.[13] The alarm was so general, said one Massachusetts member, that the city was "especially bare of ladies from abroad." This same nervous Republican stalwart prudently secured an asylum for his wife and daughter with Baron Edouard de Stoeckl, the Russian Minister, "in case the rebels pushed into Washington," a catastrophe which he was fully "prepared each morning to see."[14] After a few days at Brown's Hotel, a popular haven for Southerners, the wife of the head of the Virginia delegation noted that "here you can realize more than anywhere else the distracted state of the country."[15]

Arriving delegates merely reflected the apprehension which had prevailed for at least two months. "The terror here among the inhabitants is something wonderful to witness," testified supercilious young Henry Adams, who, stimulated by "a continual intoxication," confessed to feeling "strong and quiet in all this row."[16] Late in December, Senator Seward had warned President-elect Abraham Lincoln of a plot to seize the Capitol; and even more high-pitched warnings went to Springfield from Horace Greeley, radical editor of the *New York Tribune,* and from Major David Hunter, who urged the assembly of a hundred thousand Republican Wide-Awakes.[17] Joseph Medill of the *Chicago Tribune* talked knowingly of a Southern army converging on Washington, and promptly initiated a tradition for his paper by proclaiming himself "a volunteer sentinel on the walls."[18] With the stiffening of the Buchanan administration in early January, Joseph Holt, the new Secretary of War, initiated steps designed to inspire a greater confidence and fears subsided somewhat. But as late as a week before the Peace Conference, Congressman Elihu B. Washburne of Illinois was again advising Lincoln of "a wide spread and powerful conspiracy"; and Edwin M. Stanton, the new and militantly Unionist Attorney General from Pennsylvania, did *"not think it probable, hardly possible"* that Northern officials would still be in the Capitol on March 4.[19]

Though enfeebled by dropsy and vertigo and too stout to get astride a horse, General in Chief of the Army Winfield Scott had bestirred himself sufficiently in December to move his headquarters from New York to Washington; and by February 4 Old Fuss and Feathers, as he was called, planned the deployment of some seven hundred troops in strategic locations throughout the city.[20] More were on their way, and local contractors hurried to build the neces-

sary barracks and stables. Hastily summoned troops from Fort
Hamilton, Fort Leavenworth, and West Point bedded down in the
Columbian Armory at the intersection of Pennsylvania and Louisiana avenues, in temporary quarters near City Hall, and in barracks
on Capitol Hill near B Street, where mud was so deep guns nearly
mired. A light artillery company of ninety men found themselves
with a battery of four cannon in the unfamiliar surroundings of a
select ladies' boarding school near the War Department.

From his headquarters in Winder's Building on Seventeenth
Street, the aging Virginia-born General enforced a rigid discipline
which kept encampments free of unauthorized persons.[21] Senator
Simon Cameron of Pennsylvania, the prospective Secretary of War,
assured Lincoln that "the old warrior is roused" and "equal to the
occasion." Newspaper rumors told of attempts to poison his horses
and of "reckless scoundrels from Mississippi and South Carolina"
bent on his assassination. Secessionists complained of Scott's per-
sistence, and talked sarcastically of a pleasant inauguration day—
a "nice time for women, fashion and crinoline." Radical Republicans, on the other hand, took delight in knowing that "grinning
artillery" was ready "to rattle grape, if necessary." The *Chicago
Tribune* thought this a "charming medicine" for "the disease called
treason." "The only Peace Conference that we want," said the
*New York Tribune,* "is the one now assembled in Washington under command of Gen. Scott."[22]

Caught up in the military spirit, volunteer militiamen thronged
to sign muster rolls in units of congenial political complexion, each
preparing to defend his particular ideology by mastering close-
order drill. Catering to public demand, G. G. Evans' Bookstore announced recent shipments of a large number of military works,
including Hardee's *Rifle and Infantry* and Scott's *Infantry Tactics.*
Wall, Stephens, and Company offered great inducements to companies wishing outfits, promising "every facility in style and
prices," plus military overcoats "as low as $6." At least four units
had scheduled drill for the evening of February 4. The commander
of the National Volunteers, whose loyalty was suspect, demanded
punctual attendance and promised business of the highest importance.[23]

While politicians and editors argued over the necessity for military display, a select committee of the House of Representatives in-

vestigated the "conspiracy to seize the Federal Capital." Chief among its witnesses was Mayor James E. Berret who swore he knew nothing about it, despite widespread fears that his own police force "would most likely be . . . the aiders, abettors—chief assistants—of the invading rowdy horde." Authorities searched the old gas house on Maine Avenue, but found nothing despite whisperings that it held "a depository of arms for treasonable purposes." Citizens despairing of help from Mayor Berret organized extra-legal patrols in hopes of "putting an end to the incendiarism so rife" in various parts of the city. Fourteen men were added to the Capitol Police; a stand of arms was provided Capitol watchmen; and plans were under way to supply loyal employees with Colt's revolvers.[24] Detecting in these precautions a change in the political wind, the editor of the Washington *Constitution* announced the discontinuance of his paper, hoping to resume publication "in the more congenial atmosphere of the southern republic." "There was," said the Baltimore *American* with more hope than confidence, "too much patriotic oxygen in the air of Washington to sustain it."[25]

Peace Conference delegates found Washington an unlikely setting for peaceful negotiation. Signs of contentious strife were everywhere. In Willard's lobby, Chandler, the concessionaire, kept "cockades of all kinds—suitable for all shades of political sentiment." Former President John Tyler of Virginia described an "atmosphere where lunacy . . . prevails."[26] Southerners particularly resented the parading of United States troops, whose presence they regarded "as a menace and a threat on the part of the North." Many Northern delegates, on the other hand, looked upon the city as a nest of traitors, and found cause to suspect each individual with a Southern accent. A Massachusetts member fully expected to find rebel flags flying and the Treasury sacked. The telegraph offices, he was sure, were "filled with 'secesh.' "[27] A Vermonter with a puritanical aversion to big-city mores complained of Southern conspirators who frequented miserable hotels and "smoke begrimed rooms" inappropriately "dignified with the title of *saloon.*" Many like-minded New Englanders were horrified by the lawless discharge of firearms, to say nothing of threatened resorts to "hostile collision" between Southern senators.[28]

Moderates both North and South hoped that the assembling conferees would be equal to their appointed task. Of the 132 who eventually arrived from twenty-one states to take seats in the Conference, some owed their appointments to their respective governors, others to their legislatures; but all held official credentials duly certified by administrative authorities in the several states. "The Convention which framed our present Constitution," said one procompromise journalist, "had no more ability and less reputation among its members at the time it sat."[29] Included on the roll were a former president of the United States, six former cabinet members, nineteen former governors, fourteen former United States senators, fifty former congressmen, five former ministers or ambassadors, ten circuit judges, and twelve state supreme court justices. One hundred and three were lawyers; sixty-one had once served in their respective state legislatures; many were prominent old-line Whigs. Eleven members had served with Lincoln in the Thirtieth Congress, and five of the Southern delegates had sat with him on the Whig side of the aisle.

Heading the list of delegates were septuagenarians scarred by a lifetime of acrimonius political warfare. A great center of attraction was the seventy-one-year-old former President, John Tyler, who had retired to his plantation, Sherwood Forest, on the banks of the James River in the Virginia Tidewater on his departure from the presidency in 1845. With an unbecoming lack of modesty, Mrs. Tyler confided that her husband's "superiority over everybody else is felt and admitted by all." "Everybody," she reported, "says he is looked to to save the Union." Friendly observers noted his "animal vigor," his "keen and gentle eyes," and pictured him as "well preserved," bearing his "great age with remarkable grace." "He is," said the *Louisville Democrat,* "the same slim, tall-looking, highbread [sic] Virginia gentleman." Unsympathetic delegates, however, told of a "tottering ashen ruin," a man "more cordially despised" than any one "who ever occupied the Presidential chair."[30] Northerners suspected his secessionist tendencies, and their suspicions were not allayed when dispatches from Montgomery described the Confederate flag-raising ceremonies. The day the Conference assembled, "Captain" Tyler's granddaughter raised the Stars and Bars on the cupola of the Southern Capitol.[31]

Old Whig contemporaries shared center stage with the patrician of Sherwood Forest. John C. Wright, onetime advisor to President William Henry Harrison, though now a feeble patriarch almost blind, made the arduous midwinter trip from Cincinnati with his son, Crafts, determined to sacrifice his life, if necessary, to achieve "justice to all sections of the Union."[32] The Old Duke, Charles A. Wickliffe of Bardstown, Kentucky, onetime governor of his state and Tyler's Postmaster General, crippled since his last term in Congress in the early thirties, climaxed a lifetime of angry disputation with a sincere attempt at conciliation. The impressive and genial Silver Gray, Francis Granger, once a radical antislavery politician who resigned from Tyler's Cabinet in 1841, now advocated compromise in a divided New York delegation. Thomas Ewing, "the Old Salt Boiler of the Kanawah," who sat in the cabinets of Tyler and Zachary Taylor, came from retirement in Lancaster, Ohio, to plead for concession from both sides.[33] Reverdy Johnson of Baltimore, Maryland, Attorney General in Taylor's Cabinet, and defense attorney in Dred Scott's case, interrupted a lucrative law practice to strive for a conciliatory adjustment. The venerable William C. Rives of Castle Hill near Charlottesville, Virginia, twice minister to France, and onetime leader of Old Dominion Conservatives, joined this "solemn family council" with the high resolve of placing the Union "on a more solid footing than ever."[34]

Adding a more strident tone to the conversations at Willard's were names long identified with extreme positions and ambitious young Republicans with none of the sentimental nationalism of old-line Whiggery: David Wilmot of Pennsylvania, author of the famous antislavery Proviso; Roger S. Baldwin, former governor of Connecticut, and an antislavery lawyer in the celebrated *Amistad* case; George S. Boutwell, former governor of Massachusetts, and an inflexible favorite of Senator Charles Sumner; David Dudley Field of New York, formerly an antislavery Democrat, who in 1847 initiated the "Corner-Stone" resolution declaring uncompromising hostility to the extension of slavery; Senator William Pitt Fessenden of Maine, later described by Lincoln as "a Radical without the petulant and vicious fretfulness of many Radicals";[35] and the most pompous, if not to say most imposing, Salmon P. Chase, formerly governor of Ohio, and soon to become the radical leader in Lincoln's Cabinet.

Representatives of Northern and Southern business interests, particularly railroad interests, found many fellow delegates with similar preoccupations. Among the businessmen were: William E. Dodge, of Phelps, Dodge and Company, dealing in copper, lumber, and railroads; Valentine B. Horton, president of the Ohio River Salt Company; Caleb Blood Smith of the Cincinnati and Chicago Railroad and prospective Secretary of the Interior; John M. Forbes, a leading promoter of the Michigan Central; Erastus Corning, president of the New York Central; Reuben Hitchcock of the Cleveland and Mahoning; Benjamin Williamson of the Raritan and Delaware; James Guthrie, president of the Louisville and Nashville; Thomas Martin, president of the Nashville and Decatur; John M. Morehead, promotor of the Atlantic and North Carolina; William H. Stephens, promotor of the Mobile and Ohio, and James C. Stone, president of the Leavenworth, Pawnee and Western.

Colorful personalities gave the assembly a certain glamour. Among the more prominent characters were: Colonel Alexander W. Doniphan of Missouri, leader of a famous Mexican War expedition which covered 5,600 miles in twelve months without benefit of quartermaster, paymaster, or military discipline; General John E. Wool, Commander of the Department of the East, who was even older than General Scott; Commander Robert F. Stockton, Captain of the *Princeton* on that fatal day when the whole Tyler administration was almost blown to eternity; Stephen Trigg Logan of Illinois, Lincoln's onetime law partner and "the most thorough and accomplished lawyer" the President-elect had ever known;[36] Thomas Ruffin, Chief Justice of the North Carolina Supreme Court, and cousin of the fire-eating Edmund; former Governor Charles S. Morehead of Kentucky, the handsomest man at the Conference in the experienced eyes of Mrs. Tyler;[37] Felix Kirk Zollicoffer, pistol-toting editor and kingmaker in Tennessee politics; James A. Seddon of Virginia, uncompromising disciple of John C. Calhoun, whose gaunt frame reminded at least one observer of "an exhumed corpse after a month's interment";[38] and James B. Clay, son of the Great Compromiser, but a reluctant compromiser himself.

Unimpressed by this array of great and onetime great, Horace Greeley damned the gathering as an "Old Gentlemen's Convention" of "political fossils" disinterred only because of the shock of the secession movement. Though by no means deserving of Greeley's vitriolic abuse, members were manifestly mature statesmen.

Only seven were under forty. Twelve had survived their allotted three-score years and ten; thirty-four had reached sixty; and seventy-four were fifty or over. "These venerable old gentlemen," concluded the *Tribune,* "are no more fit to be intrusted with... guidance than a bull is fitted to keep a china shop." Secessionists held an equal contempt for this "experiment of a Peace Congress," confidently hoping it would "prove abortive." But among conservative men everywhere, as the *Cincinnati Enquirer* discerned, the Conference was "the hope of the country."[39]

## Chapter Two

# Wide-Awakes and Minute-Men

Conservatives looked upon the Peace Conference as a last resort, for both north and south of the Ohio, extremists were making the psychological and military preparations for an "irrepressible conflict." "I cannot comprehend the madness of the times," complained old-line Whig Tom Corwin in a letter to the President-elect. "Southern men are theoretically crazy. Extreme Northern men are practical fools. The latter are really quite as mad as the former." "Treason is in the air around us *every* where," concluded the onetime governor of Ohio, demonstrating an appreciation of semantics. "It goes by the name of patriotism."[1] After a trip through New England, Carl Schurz, a radical Republican lecturer, noted "the symptoms of a rising fighting spirit." "It will be an easy thing," he assured Lincoln, "if matters are well managed by our papers and public men, to lead this spirit into the proper channel."[2] Advocates of a preventive war sanguinely opined that "one campaign in the slave states would settle the matter." Some even felt it "might be finished before haying time."[3] The Secretary of the Illinois Republican State Central Committee promised partisans that Lincoln would "maintain the integrity of the union if it costs enough blood to fill Charleston harbor."[4] With an equal determination, the President-elect of the Confederacy promised to make all obstructionists "smell Southern powder and feel Southern steel."[5]

Throughout the Lower South preparations were under way to give tangible support to the military pretensions of Mr. Davis. Indeed, even before the Republican victory, fire-eaters were urging every community to supply itself with munitions. *"Let the boys arm,"* advised the editor of the Montgomery *Mail, "Everyone that can point a shotgun or revolver should have one. . . . Abolition is at your doors, with torch and knife in hand."* Followers of former Governor Henry A. Wise of Virginia raised secession poles, organized committees of safety, and mustered an ever growing corps of Minute-Men. "Don't delay a moment," the fiery secessionist warned. "Arm and drill!" Minute-Men marched behind the states' rights flag in the Deep South, and units flourished along the border as well. Led by the most influential citizens, according to the secessionist Charleston *Mercury,* these companies embraced "the flower of the youth."[6]

Within a fortnight after Lincoln's election, Southern legislatures made funds available for suitable weapons, Georgia appropriating $1,000,000, while South Carolina contented itself with $100,000. By the end of November, Northern editors were alarmed by the shipments of munitions bound for Southern ports. Late in December, South Carolina troops occupied the Federal Arsenal at Charleston and the abandoned Fort Moultrie. January brought daily reports headlining the seizure of "government works" in the Lower South. On February 18, General David E. Twiggs delivered up "thirteen hundred thousand dollars worth of public property" to secessionist officials in Texas.[7] Meanwhile, wild celebrations and one-hundred-gun salvos had greeted formal ordinances of secession in South Carolina (December 20), Mississippi (January 9), Florida (January 10), Alabama (January 11), Georgia (January 19), Louisiana (January 26), and Texas (February 1).

States of the Upper South showed greater deliberation. In December, the North Carolina Assembly rejected a resolution calling for a secession convention; but in spite of this evidence of cautious Unionism, Governor John W. Ellis worked to put the Tar Heel State on a war footing.[8] Convinced that Lincoln would pursue a coercion policy, Ellis urged legislators to be "prepared to meet Such a condition of affairs."[9] A Military Commission was established, provision was made to enroll a volunteer corps of 20,000 in case of invasion, and $300,000 was appropriated for arms.[10] The same legislation which sent commissioners to the Peace Conference dispatched observers to Montgomery—just in case.

Despite its Conditional Unionist majority, even Virginia looked to its defenses. When the General Assembly convened in January, members rushed through "An Act to Create an Ordnance Department," and asked Governor John Letcher for a plan to reconstruct the militia in accordance with a suggestion in his inaugural. A self-appointed agent in New York offered to furnish the Governor reliable intelligence of Northern military movements for a fee of fifteen or twenty dollars *per diem,* and an imaginative armchair strategist urged him to fit up "a few McCormick's Reapers" which Old Dominion troops might use to mow down Republican Wide-Awakes in Washington on March 4.[11] Discouraged Virginia conservatives testified that public sentiment was growing more depraved, every day. "The desire of some for change," noted one astute observer, "the greed of many for excitement, and the longing of more for anarchy and confusion, seem to have unthroned the reason of men, and left them at the mercy of passion and of madness."[12]

While governors readied weapons, fire-eating propagandists manipulated symbols designed to arouse citizens to the necessity for their use, a persuasive task made easy by vivid memories of John Brown and Hinton Rowan Helper. "The time for compromises is past," thundered secessionist Congressman Laurence M. Keitt at a South Carolina rally. "Let us unfurl the flag, and with the sword of State, cut the bonds of this accursed Union."[13] The impending struggle would of course be a victorious one, since Yankee courage, like that of Bob Acres, oozed out at the fingers' ends.[14] Palmetto State orators marshaled their most lurid adjectives to describe Black Republicans and the newly-elected President and Vice-President, "a Southern renegade—spewed out of the bosom of Kentucky into Illinois—and a Northern white-washed or octoroon mulatto." The Honorable Robert Barnwell Rhett, editor of the Charleston *Mercury,* daydreamed extravagantly about conquests "over Mexico—over the isles of the sea—over the far off Southern tropics." "The long weary night of our oppression and danger is passing away," he announced magniloquently, "and the glorious dawn of a Southern Confederacy breaks in our view."[15]

From the explosive origins in South Carolina, reverberations sounded throughout the Lower South. Howell Cobb of Georgia, John B. Floyd of Virginia, and Jacob Thompson of Mississippi, disunionist members of Buchanan's Cabinet, resigned late in December to set off secession fireworks back home.[16] Even while still Secretary of the Interior, Thompson journeyed to Raleigh as a Mississippi commissioner charged with the responsibility of persuading North Carolina to act for the common defense and safety of the South.[17] Amid derisive jeers in the Senate, Louis T. Wigfall of Texas heralded the economic advantages of separation by proclaiming "Cotton is King" and predicting a direct trade of 250 millions for Southern ports. In Alabama, William L. Yancey talked fiercely about the imperative duty of Cotton State citizens to protect their honor.[18] In an invitational appearance before the Georgia Legislature, United States Senator Robert Toombs begged members to arm him with "the sword." "If you do not," he cried, "...as God lives, I will take it for myself."[19] Such turgid pronouncements distended Yankee eardrums, but often failed to convey credibility. "The tendency of slaveholders who can read and write," said Horace Greeley contemptuously, "seems to be to muddle themselves with cheap metaphysics, and to flounder in a slough of dubious dialectics."[20]

Religious leaders mobilized the Deity. Picturing "the unchristian aggressions of the North," an Episcopalian divine in New Orleans called forth "the hand of God" to protect "his ordained institutions."[21] A leading Southern Baptist described the conflict as a divine mission against fanaticism, "the product of infidelity, of [a] rebellion against God that presumes to be wiser than the Scriptures." The Presbyterian Synod of South Carolina called upon its members to imitate their Revolutionary forefathers, while reminding Christians of their duty to God, as well as to their ancestors, their children, and their slaves. The Reverend Christopher P. Gadsden of Charleston's St. Luke's Church preached a sermon which the *New York Tribune* described as an hysterical "ecclesiastico-military hash" of "prayer and powder and Palmetto flags, Bibles and bayonets, the sword of steel and the sword of the spirit."[22]

With hysteria came the suppression of Unionist sentiment and attacks on Northern merchants and travelers. Correspondents found it "more than ordinarily hazardous for Northern people to breathe the air of the South." Visitors described as abolitionists were arrested daily in New Orleans, and from Memphis came word that "no Northern man is safe in the South now." An anonymous observer in Charleston described "a system of espionage more tyrannous than ever prevailed in Austria." "Vigilance Committees are everywhere," said this covert agent for Greeley's *Tribune.* "Nothing is allowed that does not pander to the insane ideas of the times." Opponents of secession were damned as submissionists, and it became increasingly difficult to advise moderation. The pro-Unionist speech of Senator Alexander H. Stephens was not permitted to circulate in South Carolina and was "very widely suppressed" in Georgia. Most moderates lacked the flamboyant courage of Parson William G. Brownlow, who, when threatened with hanging by secessionists, designated the appropriate day, invited the public, and promised a speech under the gallows.[23] In describing the prevailing repression, a Tennessee Unionist told of a reign of terror. "Freedom," he declared, "is shrieking her expiring agonies here."[24]

North of the Ohio, Yankee radicals prepared to meet the Dixie challengers. Indeed, many cheered the thought of a "good hearty fight on or about the 4th of March." Horace White of the *Chicago Tribune* told Lincoln of a multitude ready to "plunge into blood to the horses['] bridles to defend your newly acquired prerogatives."[25] Radical Congressmen pressed for a force bill reminiscent of that passed under President Andrew Jackson during the nullification crisis. On December 23, Republican "ultras" of both houses met in the Washington quarters of Francis P. Blair, Sr., and "unanimously agreed that the integrity of the Union should be preserved, though it cost a million lives."[26] Among this group were those afflicted with what one conservative Republican diagnosed as a Yankee type of secession fever: Congressman Elihu B. Washburne of Illinois, who supported bold and decisive action;[27] Senator James R. Doolittle of Wisconsin, who solemnly promised Lincoln, "I will not consent [to compromise], though the grave should open this very hour";[28] and Senator Charles Sumner of Massachusetts, who explained, "How easily it would be for me to give my life rather then [*sic*] here take a single backward step."[29] In January, Edward Everett, onetime President of Harvard, visited Sumner and found him in "a state of morbid excitement approaching to insanity."[30]

When South Carolina troops opened fire on a federal supply ship for Fort Sumter on January 9, conservative Republican Thurlow Weed thought it a favorable omen, while radicals morbidly hoped for blood.[31] "If only they've hurt some one on the Star of the West," exulted Henry Adams, son of Lincoln's Minister to England. "It will raise the North to fever heat and perhaps secure Kentucky." "The truth is a good deal depends for us on a little bit of a fight," Adams admitted in a letter to his brother. "If Major Anderson and his whole command were all murdered in cold blood, it would be an excellent thing for the country, much as I should regret it on the part of those individuals."[32] "If it cannot be prevented otherwise," blustered an advisor of Governor John Andrew of Massachusetts, "let us drive the ruffians into the Gulf of Mexico and give the country to the negroes."[33]

Fortified by declarations of this sort, Republican governors nervously surveyed their respective militias and found them in wretched states of disrepair. Governors Israel Washburn of Maine, Edwin D. Morgan of New York, Andrew G. Curtin of Pennsylvania, John Andrew of Massachusetts, and William Dennison of Ohio met in New York City and resolved to be ready to maintain the Constitution and to enforce the law at all hazards.[34] Adjutants general in Michigan and Pennsylvania promised Lincoln support in any emergency.[35] Governor Erastus Fairbanks of Vermont recommended that his fellow executives undertake "a vigorous and imposing organization of the militia."[36] Such advice was hardly needed by his neighbors Andrew and Morgan, both of whom were preparing to offer troops to General Scott. Andrew, in fact, was devoting himself to the logistics of moving the Massachusetts militia to the nation's capital.[37] Though fearful of calling militiamen to Washington because of "hurtful jealousies," Scott nevertheless urged state officials "to look up their arms and have them taken care of." Governor Morgan, he felt, might well have "a force of 5,000 to 10,000 men in readiness at forty eight or even twenty four hours notice"; and in conveying this message, Senator Seward warned that there should be "no publicity of such a purpose."[38]

Irrepressible Republican governors in Illinois and Indiana were emboldened by the increased martial spirit reflected in their correspondence, but recalcitrant state legislatures retarded them in the refurbishing of their militia. Correspondents of Governor Yates urged an immediate enrollment, and Horace White reported that "everybody" in Chicago was signing petitions for decisive action.[39]

"It may be essentially necessary," advised the excitable Joseph Medill, "for a dozen or twenty of our Illinois volunteer companies to be fully prepared to start on a day[']s notice for Baltimore and Washington."[40] Congressman Washburne felt that not a day should be lost in putting the state on a war footing.[41] In spite of these entreaties, January passed without legislative action. Impatient with the delay, Governor Yates on his own initiative took steps to obtain arms from Washington and to ensure the safety of the St. Louis Arsenal.[42] In Indiana, Democrats in the Legislature stubbornly blocked appropriations for the milita by bolting the sessions, thereby preventing the quorum necessary to enable Republicans to pass legislation. Undaunted, Governor Oliver P. Morton salvaged inferior weapons rusting in state armories and persistently appealed to Washington for more.[43]

Not all Northern military preparations were undertaken by legally constituted authority. Radical members of Republican campaign marching clubs, the Wide-Awakes, relieved the postelection boredom by perfecting their close-order drill and by striving to regulate the thinking of their less belligerent fellow citizens. Some of these self-appointed guardians of the national safety were provided with arms, and the indefatigable Carl Schurz suggested a plan whereby "volunteer-companies all over the north" might be mustered to the federal colors "in the regular way."[44] An army major gratuitously advised Lincoln to "have a hundred thousand Wide Awakes wend their way quietly to Washington, during the first three days of March."[45] It was apparent that many were ready to set out. A Wide-Awake in Hartford, Connecticut, promised Lincoln a thousand men, or any reasonable number, *organized & armed.* A somewhat less ambitious New Yorker tendered "the Services of One hundred able bodied Men," none of whom weighed less than 150 pounds.[46] "Our wide awakes," testified one Illinoisan confidently, "are ready to grasp the rifle and march down to that tory nest if need be."[47]

Exhorting Wide-Awakes to derring-do were radicals like Horace Greeley who adopted a stridently anticompromise policy after toying briefly with the idea of letting the erring sisters go in peace. Fearful that a compromise would "consummate the suicide" of the Republican party, Greeley headlined a daily column NO NEGOTIATIONS WITH TRAITORS. "Another nasty compromise," he told Lincoln, ". . . will so strongly disgrace and humiliate us that we can

never again raise our heads."[48] Former Governor Chase agreed
with this inflexible position, firmly appraising the danger of ideological capitulation "greater still and more imminent" than seizure
of the Capitol.[49] Irrepressibles liked the compromise of Ohio's
Bluff Ben Wade, who demanded 200 traitors for hanging and
magnanimously agreed to a conciliatory adjustment of 150.[50]
Rather than become "the mere serfs of an arrogant . . . minority of
negro-breeders," Wisconsin radicals welcomed civil war "with all
its accompaniments of horror."[51] "I hope all compromises may end
in smoke," declared one pugnacious Westerner, "even should it
be the smoke of the cannon and the battlefield."[52]

Radical bravado flourished at the verbal level, with few if any
anticipating a prolonged or bloody conflict. "There may be some
bloodshed," said one editor stoically, "but it won't be much."[53]
Even the more realistic Joseph Medill felt confident that all would
be settled in two years. "If we can keep Maryland loyal," he
opined, "it will not be hard to thrash the rest of niggerdom."[54]
Seward warned the President-elect that, despite the reckless position of the "largest portion" of his party, the North would not
consent to a long civil war.[55] Sumner could scarcely conceal his
glee at any mention of war's inevitability; those less overtly warlike
talked sanctimoniously of sparing their children.[56] In evaluating
Western sentiment, Lincoln's law partner, William H. Herndon, reported, "Our people here . . . say manfully[,] 'meet it now, and
[do] not hand it down to our posterity. . . .' "[57]

The lazy-minded had their thinking short-circuited with slogans.
Seward's phrase, "the irrepressible conflict" gave citizens a feeling
of helpless inevitability which in itself hastened the day of mobilization. At least one Southern Unionist quoted him as saying that
such expressions were "intended for effect at home and not designed to reach the ear of the South."[58] Radical editors, unlike the
equilibristic Senator, spoke in deadly earnest, however, when they
demanded "enforcement of the laws," "the Constitution as it is,"
and "no surrender of principle." Lincoln likewise stood immovably
on the hastily constructed Chicago platform, refusing to buy or
beg for "the privilege of taking possession of the Government."[59]
After an interview in Springfield, Schurz insisted that Old Abe
was "fest wie eine mauer."[60] Though opposed to a conciliatory
settlement at any time, Chase nevertheless popularized the watchword, "Inauguration first—adjustment afterwards."[61] Like-minded

radicals talked disparagingly of weak-kneed Republicans suscepti-
ble to unmanly concessions while admonishing one another to
stand firm.[62] "We are sick of the baby-talk of 'no coercion,' 'no
shedding of fraternal blood,' and like nonsense," exclaimed the
editor of Lincoln's favorite paper, the *Illinois State Journal.* "Treason *should* be coerced."[63]

Secessionists anticipated Lincoln's resort to coercion, confidently
hoping it would send border-state delegates scurrying to Montgomery. Radical Republicans similarly hoped for an inflexible
slaveholding stand against peaceable adjustment.[64] Ohio's frenetic
abolitionist, Joshua R. Giddings, looked to the Southerners "to do
more for us than we can do for ourselves";[65] and Gideon Welles,
the incoming Secretary of the Navy, was assured that the ultimate
escape from concessions "lies in the refusal of the South to take
them."[66] "My only hope of escaping the disgrace of compromise,"
said former Massachusetts Congressman Calvin C. Chaffee, "is in
the firmness of the seceders & fire eaters."[67] Aware of such extremist
attitudes, Senator Stephen A. Douglas came to an obvious conclusion: "Northern disunionists, like the disunionists of the South,
are violently opposed to all . . . efforts at conciliation, whereby
peace should be restored and the Union preserved."[68]

Feeling between extremist groups ran high, particularly along
the border. Rival companies of Wide-Awakes and Minute-Men
armed themselves in border-state cities; heated partisan orators
damned moderates as submissionists and Black Republicans; a
prominent Tennessee Unionist was threatened with hanging.[69] A
North Carolina editor suggested branding compromising traitors
with "a more prominent mark than was placed upon the murderer
Cain."[70] In New York City, the superintendent of police became
so incensed by inflammatory anti-Republican handbills that he
asked Governor Morgan for a law permitting indictments for treason "and kindred offenses."[71] Frightened by these ominous signs of
repression, the Democratic editor of the Albany *Atlas and Argus*
proclaimed, "The reign of Opinion has ended; and that of Force
has begun!" "If we escape the actual disintegration of our government," he predicted, "we shall have impaired the purity of our system and tainted the blood of the Republic with that leprosy of
force, whose symptoms are pain and fever within, and corroding
sores and fetid corruption . . . on the surface."[72]

## Chapter Three

# A Project to Rally
# the People

With extremists on both sides making preparations for the use of force, conservative Republicans joined with moderates of the Democratic and Constitutional Union parties in attempts at compromise through negotiation. Conservative leaders in the border states, particularly in Virginia and Kentucky, grew impatient with Congressional bickering over proposals of adjustment in the House Committee of Thirty-three and the Senate Committee of Thirteen and looked for other possible constitutional solutions of their problems. They challenged the concept of irrepressible conflict, avoiding a fatalistic attitude which placed human events beyond the control of reason. They displayed a confidence in *the people* of both sections and denounced the "perverted mediums of stump speeches, partisan diatribes, [and] buncombe resolutions." "We seriously believe," wrote George D. Prentice, editor of the *Louisville Journal,* "that when the North and the South meet each other face to face and eye to eye . . . , they will be prepared to fraternize most cordially, and kick parties, politicians, platforms and schemers into the pit of Tophet." The rival *Louisville Democrat* agreed that four-fifths of the voters favored "a fair and just compromise to save the Union of these States entire."[1]

Though a majority of Americans may have indeed favored some kind of amicable adjustment, moderates were unorganized and far less vocal than strident advocates of extreme positions. And above all they needed a rallying point on which to assemble their diverse legions. "Give us a reasonable project," exclaimed one ardent Unionist, ". . . and we will sweep the impracticables of the North out of power like a whirlwind. The people are not prepared to sustain a set of men who prefer their party to their country."[2] Conservatives looked to the Peace Conference for such a project, and throughout the border states its announcement was heralded as a favorable omen.

Proposals for a conference had been in the air since midsummer of 1860 when Governor Letcher of Virginia had first suggested one. On November 9, President Buchanan discussed such a gathering with his Cabinet; and less than a month later, William C. Rives urged "a solemn family council" in a long letter to Congressman Alexander R. Boteler, a Unionist Congressman from Virginia.[3] That same month, a group of New York merchants asked Governor Morgan to call a convention, and George D. Prentice of the *Louisville Journal* made an appeal for "such amendments to the Constitution as will correct the present deplorable and alarming derangement of our political system." Governor Beriah Magoffin of Kentucky and the Kentucky Congressional delegation endorsed Prentice's appeal, and on January 25, Magoffin signed a joint resolution by the Kentucky Legislature calling for a convention under the provisions of the fifth article of the Constitution.[4] That same week, the General Assembly of Tennessee passed a similar resolution, but proposed that delegates from all the slaveholding states should first assemble to define a basis of adjustment.[5]

Reflecting upon the madness of the times at his Sherwood Forest retreat, ex-President John Tyler likewise devised plans for a consultation between the border states. "They are most interested in keeping the peace," he wrote former Attorney General Caleb Cushing of Massachusetts, "and, if they cannot come to an understanding, then the political union is gone, as is already, to a great extent the union of fraternal feeling." In December, the onetime President looked upon such a gathering as a last resort; by mid-January, he felt it imperative that a call be issued. Consequently, on January 17, he published his proposal for a meeting of representatives from the border states, six free and six slave. Since Tyler commanded the respect of strong Southern-rights Virginians, his letter did much to minimize extremist opposition to a conference. Even the secessionist *Richmond Enquirer* urged its readers to give careful consideration to this proposal "from that noble old Roman" who during the nullification crisis had voted "solitary and alone" against Jackson's Force Bill.[6]

Although former Governor Wise thought the Conference mainly the work of Mr. Tyler, others felt that Governor Letcher and his moderate lieutenants had been more influential in bringing it about. In his message on January 7, Letcher once again recommended a convention of the states, indicating that peaceful separation from the Union should not be considered until a last attempt was made to arrive at a conciliatory adjustment.[7] James F. Johnson introduced the resolution in the Virginia Legislature and James Barbour of Culpepper rose "from the bed of sickness on which he had been laying [*sic*] for four or five months" to steer the Governor's proposal through the parliamentary shoals of disunionist opposition.[8] During the discussions in Barbour's Joint Committee on State and Federal Relations, Tyler's plan was modified to provide an invitation to "all such States, whether slaveholding or non-slaveholding, as are willing to unite with Virginia in an earnest effort to adjust present unhappy controversies."

Delegates in the House defeated a minority report which would have sent commissioners to Montgomery instead of Washington; and by a vote of 63 to 55 they also defeated a substitute resolution declaring it "a dangerous delusion to suppose the interests of Virginia are not thoroughly identified with those of her southern sisters." As the basis of an adjustment, they suggested the compromise resolutions of Senator John J. Crittenden of Kentucky— with some modifications. Tyler, the elder statesman, was sent to Washington to induce President Buchanan to agree to abstain "from any and all acts calculated to produce a collision of arms" during the proposed Conference; Judge John Robertson was given a similar mission to South Carolina and "other states that have seceded or shall secede." The date selected was February 4, the day Alabama had chosen for assembling the seceded states at Montgomery.[9]

The General Assembly chose commissioners with opposing views. Tyler and James A. Seddon were dedicated advocates of a strong Southern-rights position. George W. Summers and William C. Rives were Conditional Unionists of considerably more moderate temperament. The fifth commissioner, Judge J. W. Brockenbrough professed a catholic spirit, but nevertheless was inclined to side with Seddon. The Judge lived in Lexington, however; and his strongly Unionist neighbors talked guardedly about "applying the screws" should he decide to misrepresent them.[10]

Since he was certain that the seceding states would not participate, Tyler regretted the changes in his proposal, charging that the General Assembly had enlarged the gathering for the worse. The *Enquirer* damned the change as "a rare instance of nondescript legislation" and denounced the Legislature for giving "the enemy time—time to prepare and apply all the means of coercion." George D. Prentice, however, praised it as a harmonious action for the vindication of the Constitution and the protection of the American people, while comparing it with the Kentucky and Virginia resolutions of 1798.[11]

Virginia's invitation met with the greatest enthusiasm in those areas where the economic consequences of disunion were most feared—the border states and the Northern commercial centers. Since secession had already precipitated an economic crisis, business interests, particularly the well-established ones—banking, textiles, and commerce—looked hopefully to a speedy adjustment. As abolitionist Wendell Phillips had noted earlier, Union sentiment was fostered by "the clink of coin—the whistle of spindles, the dust of trade."[12] One Washington correspondent reported great pressure from business and "high social circles in all our great cities for compromise," and even the radical Greeley admitted that among businessmen "the desire for some compromise is strong, almost overpowering."[13]

Those engaged in Southern trade, the cottonocracy, were of course thoroughly alarmed. "The mercantile gloom that hovers over our city," said one disconsolate New Yorker, "is darker than I ever knew it, and this year now promises to be the most disastrous ever known in this country. . . ." In a melancholy report to Lincoln, Senator Lyman Trumbull of Illinois testified that "hundreds of fortunes are daily being lost." During the month of January, 466 firms failed: 112 in New York, 60 in Massachusetts, 40 in Ohio, and 29 in Pennsylvania.[14] By February 1, Virginia securities were down 40 per cent and other border-state issues suffered correspondingly. Cotton-state banks suspended payments; buyers refused to pay Yankee creditors; and Dixie entrepreneurs looked hopefully to a direct trade with Europe.[15] Desperate New Yorkers conjured up rash alternatives to offset their Southern losses: Governor Morgan urged Lincoln to consider the propriety of getting Cuba by purchase; Henry J. Raymond, editor of the *New York Times,* endorsed the idea of acquiring Mexico; others looked acquisitively northward toward Canada.[16] In his January message to the New York City Council, Mayor Fernando Wood seriously proposed setting up as "a Free City," thereby securing "the united support of the Southern states."[17]

In the excitement caused by the panic, Republicans who once staunchly supported the Chicago platform were frightened into a more conciliatory position. As one Wisconsin radical exclaimed, "There are some men whose consciences are so tender, they cannot even *look* into the face of *Mars*—but they can ogle *Venus* without a blush!"[18] Former Governor Hamilton Fish of New York observed "a very *great change* in the *tone* of *some* of our merchants who were among the most active in the Republican ranks." "Some who feared that the chosen standard bearer was not stiff enough," said Fish, "now surprise me by the extent of concessions they are anxious to make."[19] Prominent Republican capitalists begged Lincoln "to lay aside party trammels" and to offer fair terms of conciliation.[20] New York's merchant prince, Alexander T. Stewart, complained that the refusal of the radical Republicans to concede "costs us millions daily" and subjects the nation "to every conceivable mischief and danger." George D. Morgan, a cousin and the Republican business partner of the Governor, was ready to "accept the Dred Scott decision and let slavery roam wher'er [*sic*] it will over the territories." After contemplating his losses in Southern securities, Morgan regretfully concluded that "it would have promoted the peace of the country to have had Bell & Everett elected." "I... would yield much for peace," exclaimed this magnanimous stockbroker, "even if I had no interest in Missouri Bonds."[21]

Noting the tensions between these "practicable" Republicans

and their "impracticable" colleagues, waggish Democrats talked facetiously of an irrepressible conflict within the victorious party. Spokesman for the conservatives was the highly "practicable" Thurlow Weed, longtime czar of New York politics and the political godfather of Senator Seward. In an editorial in his Albany *Evening Journal* on November 24, Weed suggested restoration of the Missouri Compromise line, a stunning retreat from the Chicago platform, and a suggestion which prompted radicals to describe him as "the late leader and the present betrayer of the cause of Freedom."[22] The radical editor and sometime poet, William Cullen Bryant, denounced Weed's proposal to Lincoln, assuring him that most Republicans had a decided aversion to concessions "manufactured in Wall Street";[23] and of course Bryant received high-pitched support from Horace Greeley, David Dudley Field, Senator Preston King, and "Republicans of *Democratic* antecedents." Carl Schurz, for example, suggested impeaching Buchanan to take the public mind off compromise.[24]

Henry J. Raymond of the *New York Times,* however, defended Weed in his concern for conciliation, and an active conservative group rallied around the Albany Boss.[25] Dismayed to find Republican ranks wavering under "the manipulations of Lord Thurlow," radicals intensified their efforts to stiffen the fainthearted.[26]

Businessmen likewise bestirred themselves. Convinced that the re-establishment of fraternal relations was essential for the return of prosperity, a committee of bankers and merchants in New York City secured 38,000 signatures on a petition supporting compromise. An impressive group delivered this 1,200-foot document to Congress and arranged a supper at Willard's for some seventy Republican Congressmen. Senator James Dixon of Connecticut thought the pressure of such lobbying great enough to make it "impossible for men to exercise their own judgement."[27] Overawed by the event, radical Samuel Ryan Curtis of Iowa admitted that even some "impracticables" assured their hosts they were "not so unreasonable as some had made them to believe."[28] Senator Seward did his bit by presenting the petition to the Senate; but his speeches, though conciliatory in tone, offered nothing in the way of adjustment. "If I were a disunionist," said one radical, "I should say there was cats['] claws in all that soft fur." Greeley was nevertheless enraged at Seward's speech of presentation and headlined his account in the *Tribune,* MR. SEWARD ABANDONS THE REPUBLICAN PARTY.[29]

In Boston, a similar group of influential businessmen secured over 14,000 signatures on one compromise petition and an additional 22,000 on another which circulated throughout the state. Both were carried to Washington late in January by a distinguished delegation including former Speaker of the House Robert C. Winthrop, textile manufacturer Amos A. Lawrence, and Edward Everett, the Constitutional Union candidate for Vice-President in 1860. Though the petition was wrapped in the American flag, Senator Sumner charged that it did not represent the opinions of his constituents. In retaliation, the Boston Common Council censured the Senator for his remarks. Shortly after dispatching the petition, Boston financiers met at the Merchants' Exchange to urge that Massachusetts accept Virginia's invitation to the Peace Conference.[30]

Fearful that perhaps petitions and dinners were not sufficiently persuasive, some New York bankers reportedly threatened not "to accommodate the Government with a loan" unless they received pledges of a negotiated adjustment. "The vaults of these obdurate gentlemen," said the *New York Times* disapprovingly, "shall shed not a single coin until Government, in the plenitude of its penitence, shall hold out the olive branch to its rebellious subjects, and give peace to the people." Obviously, money changers wrongfully intruded upon the democratic temple—even in the view of the conservative Raymond, who complimented the capitalists of Boston for promptly repudiating this senseless threat. Radicals denounced the scheme as a humbug and made plans to counteract it by selling government securities to states and to the public generally. "If the new administration can start with a full supply of the sinews of war," said one radical hopefully, "it will...make it wholly unnecessary to call a special session of Congress merely for the purpose of raising money."[31]

Though few, if any, groups could exert more influence than the combination of Boston and New York capitalists, conservatives nevertheless found widespread public support outside the great commercial centers. Doughface Buchanan Democrats advocated Southern rights as a longstanding matter of fundamental principle; Douglas Squatter Sovereignty Democrats were now prepared to make "any sacrifice consistent with patriotism" to save the Republic; Constitutional Unionists, like their standard-bearer, John Bell of Tennessee, resolved to adhere to the Union and to exhaust every constitutional means for the redress of grievances. If the election figures of 1860 were any indication, conservative forces had a majority in the North, as well as in the South. Senators Crittenden and Douglas were deluged with petitions and testimonials in favor of conciliation.[32] "You have the eternal gratitude of *thousands* of Young Democrats north of Mason & Dixon," testified a Crittenden correspondent, "who will *fight* for you & your *Compromise to the death*."[33]

Strong procompromise feeling prevailed along the border, particularly in the river towns of Cincinnati, Louisville, and St. Louis, where ties of trade as well as sentiment enhanced the love of Union. South of the National Road in Ohio, Indiana, and Illinois, business arrangements depended upon a lively hog and hominy market in the South. Arteries of commerce gave the central region a certain economic unity: the Louisville and Nashville, Illinois Central, and Baltimore and Ohio railroads, as well as the Cumberland, Tennessee, Ohio, and Mississippi rivers.[34] Railroad and real estate entrepreneurs of course had hopes for federal help with a Pacific railroad along a central route which might contribute still more to the economic prosperity of the region, but certainly no one wanted a hostile power interfering with communication southward. "If it *should* be necessary to keep the Miss River open," said one determined Hoosier, "the North West will attend to that."[35] Rural folks, many of Southern origin, recognized kindred political bonds with farmers across the river and were dismayed at a possible loss of farm voting power in Congress. "That will be a sorry day for the people of Indiana," observed the New Albany *Ledger,* "when they sacrifice the friendship of the Southern neighbors for that of the cold and calculating Yankees and grasping Wall Street stockjobbers."[36] Once it became clear that the Ohio might become a hostile boundary, many residents—even those who had voted for Lincoln—discovered that they were amenable to conciliation.[37]

Across the river, economic panic intensified the desire for a negotiated adjustment. "The unsettled condition of the country," complained the *Louisville Democrat,* "has completely paralyzed trade everywhere."[38] Banks in Richmond, Baltimore, Washington, and St. Louis suspended species payment, and money was "very stringent."[39] Border-state traders worried about their Dixie market for hemp, tobacco, corn, bacon, whiskey, and mules. The *Louisville Democrat* charged that the chief captains in Secessia sought to make Kentucky subservient to the ambitions of South Carolina. "Charleston is to be the New York of the South," said the *Democrat,* "and Louisville is to be a little frontier town, exposed to all the evils of such a locality."[40] Slave dealers feared a secessionist plan to reopen the overseas trade, thereby restricting their market and drastically reducing prices.[41]

On the other hand, some sections of Virginia, North Carolina, Kentucky, and Tennessee were less suited to plantation conditions and less identified economically with slavery than most areas farther south. In fact, in 1850, there were fewer than 350,000 slaveholders in the country, and it was not yet certain that all classes of Southern society were ready to accept disunion in order to accommodate the wealthy few. In the Virginia Senate, Alexander Rives warned that the Old Dominion would be "seriously damaged by *the direct taxation, free trade,* and *importation of African slaves"*—"the chief aims of the Cotton States." In some counties of North Carolina, Kenneth Rayner found that "people who did not own slaves were swearing that they 'would not lift a finger to protect rich men's negroes.' " Francis P. Blair felt that even in South Carolina "the lower orders" in society might possibly "take up arms with the slaves against the masters that oppress them."[42]

Sharing a hatred for extremists on both sides of the Ohio, Southern Unionists and Conditional Unionists looked to the Peace Conference for concessions which might strengthen their position in the bitter struggle with secessionists. "The Disunionists North... shout, no compromise!" the *Louisville Democrat* noted with disgust. "They but echo the Disunion slang of the South." The St. Louis *Missouri Statesman* accused "fanatics, panic-makers, and foul spirits of both sections" with threatening to "destroy the fair fabric of our liberties."[43] The Raleigh *North Carolina Standard* thought that if five hundred extremist "public men of the two sections" could be "confined in dungeons for six months," a more glorious Union would certainly be "restored and reconstructed."[44] When the Richmond *Whig* condemned South Carolina for pursuing a suicidal course, the witty editor of the *Louisville Journal* quipped that he knew of no state that "could pursue such a course with greater advantage to mankind."[45]

Conservative border-state spokesmen begged Republicans for "some sort of *action*" which would enable them to counteract secessionist misrepresentation. Weed estimated that tens of thousands of "anxious, devoted Union men . . . asked only that they should be thrown a plank which promised a chance to safety."[46] Though the Albany Boss was eager to answer these desperate pleas, he found "less disposition to harmonize" among his Republican colleagues. Seward called border-state appeals "very painful" because of a pervasive fear that without Republican concessions "these states must all go with the tide."[47] With concessions, however, and "the ultimate success of the Peace Conference," optimistic Southern conservatives predicted that secessionists would be "buried so deep that the hand of insurrection can never reach them."[48]

## Chapter Four

# Matters of Political Necessity

Virginia's invitation to the Peace Conference initiated bitter legislative battles in most Northern states. Republican governors exchanged hurried telegrams in an attempt to follow a common policy; and since Lincoln was reportedly advising Governor Richard Yates, many looked to see what Illinois would do. Governors Israel Washburn of Maine and William Dennison of Ohio urged Yates to refuse acceptance—at least until after Lincoln's inauguration. Fearing "nothing so much... as this new Congress," Washburn warned that the appointment of delegates "would demoralize the Republican Party."[1]

Governor Oliver P. Morton of Indiana, on the other hand, thought Illinois should accept as "a measure of prudence." Though he shared Washburn's fears, the astute Hoosier radical felt it wiser to send delegates who would "operate as a powerful restraint upon any disposition... to compromise the integrity and future of the Republican party." He explained his strategy in a letter to the President-elect:

If the Republican party of a great state like Pennsylvania should go over to the Crittenden proposition or any other of a similar character it would operate greatly to disorganize the party in every other; to detach a portion of it large enough to destroy its power. The Union feeling is very strong—*it is stronger than any party;* and when a Convention like that proposed by Virginia is called to devise measures ostensibly to save the Union, it might be better to take hold of it and control it, than to stand by and suffer the consequences of its action when we have had no share in moulding it.[2]

Speaking for the conservatives, New York's Thurlow Weed saw still another reason for Republican participation. "Virginia can be held awhile," he assured Lincoln, "if the Free States send commissioners. . . ."[3]

Divided counsel from outside made it no easier for Illinois Republicans to come to a decision on Virginia's controversial proposal, and angry voices were heard inside the Republican caucus room in Springfield. The radical editor of the *Illinois State Journal* thought the Governor should "hardly trouble himself" to appoint commissioners when "such extreme concessions to the slave power" constituted the only object of the Conference. Elected officials, however, took alarm at severe outside pressure for some conciliatory action by Republicans in the Legislature. As State Senator William Jayne sarcastically observed, "Some of our friends are getting very anxious to save the Union." To resolve the controversy, Yates sought the opinion of the President-elect who advised "not at present to take any action." "Lincoln said," according to report, "that he would rather be hung by the neck til he was dead on the steps of the Capitol, before he would buy or beg a peaceful inauguration."[4]

Bolstered by this pronouncement, Republican legislators held two tense caucuses on the evenings of January 30 and 31. Two important visitors attended the first meeting: Edward Bates of Missouri, soon to become Lincoln's Attorney General, and John Palmer Usher of Indiana, who later became Lincoln's Secretary of the Interior. Although the moderate Mr. Bates may have served as a steadying influence, it was Usher who made the decisive point against Lincoln's proposed policy of non-participation. Unless "our friends" "take hold" and appoint "men of our own," he argued, "enough of our conservatives" will unite with the Democrats to "appoint men who would misrepresent the State."[5] Since Democrats warmly endorsed the Peace Conference, defection of but a few Republican legislators in each Northern state might send a conciliatory majority to Washington. To avoid this possibility, Illinois Republicans decided to push through a resolution giving the Governor power to appoint commissioners. A radical legislator clearly explained the awkward situation to Senator Trumbull: "The proposition...was passed...as a matter of political necessity—because if we had not united to do so, some of our knock kneed brethren, would have united with the democracy, and would have given them sufficient strength to have carried the resolutions appointing by the General Assembly."[6]

In making the appointments, Governor Yates consulted all Republican factions and influences, including State Auditor Jesse K. Dubois and State Treasurer William Butler, each of whom apparently had a voice in the matter. Radicals delighted in the selection of former Governor John Wood and former State Senator Burton C. Cook. Nor were they displeased with John M. Palmer, a onetime anti-Nebraska Democrat who replaced former Lieutenant Governor Gustave Koerner in the delegation when Koerner declined to serve because he "had nothing to compromise." Though the *New York Times* characterized all the delegates as "decided anti-compromise Republicans," many Illinois radicals expressed concern over Judge Stephen T. Logan and Thomas J. Turner. Dubois and Butler preferred David Davis, but Yates obstinately persisted in the appointment of Turner, who, it was claimed, had "neither ability or respectability." When presented with a note of complaint on this, Lincoln scrawled a hasty reply: "Do not think any objection to Turner of enough importance to have a squabble over."[7]

So that no one would interpret the dispatch of delegates as an indication of weakness, the Legislature explicitly stated that the appointment of a commission did not mean an approval of the basis of settlement proposed by Virginia. "We do not like the idea of *buying* the right to control the offices which the people have given the Republicans," said the militant editor of the *Illinois State Journal,* echoing the President-elect.[8]

Meanwhile, Republicans in other states were arguing over Virginia's embarrassing invitation. In Indiana, radicals worried about the very real possibility of a conservative coalition, since presumably "two-thirds at least—more likely *three-fourths*" of the voters favored "the Crittenden or any similar proposition."[9] "Our only fear here," confessed the Speaker of the Indiana House of Representatives, "is that some of our men will commit us [to a procompromise delegation] hoping to make a little personal capital." Like most radicals, Speaker Cyrus M. Allen was positive nothing would come of the convocation, but he nevertheless acquiesced to the wishes of those colleagues who thought time might be gained by holding the border states until the day of the inauguration. Expediency thus dictated a delegation appointed by the inflexible Governor Morton, who thought it wiser to control the gathering rather "than to stand by and suffer the consequences."[10] After several wordy encounters and a bloodless duel between two enraged members, the Legislature formulated its instructions to Indiana delegates (1) prohibiting them from participating in the actions of the Conference until nineteen states were represented, thereby guaranteeing a free-state majority, and (2) urging them to seek a postponement of the Conference to a later date. Not satisfied with these safeguards, Morton in addition asked each prospective delegate for a statement pledging opposition to any new guarantee for slavery. All were of course Republicans who felt the Conference set a "dangerous and mischievous" precedent.[11]

In Ohio, radicals parroted the editorials of Greeley's *Tribune* and denounced Virginia's conciliatory gesture as an attempt to defraud the Republican party of the legitimate results of its victory.[12] "There *is* no *compromise* possible in the nature of things," State Senator Jacob Dolson Cox asserted in a letter to Ben Wade. "For us to do it after our victory, would be to confess ourselves dastards unworthy of the name of freemen." Johnson H. Jordan wrote Senator Trumbull from Cincinnati to warn that if Republicans consented to a compromise the party "would be *smashed into a thousand fragments*." Troubled by such warnings, and not knowing that the same acrimonious controversy raged in the very anterooms of the President-elect, Governor Dennison telegraphed Springfield in the vain hope that he might receive a firm decision from that quarter.[13]

On January 30, after what was described as a considerable flurry, the Ohio General Assembly authorized Dennison to select delegates with the consent of the Senate. The suspicions of the legislators, however, were written into the resolutions. "We are not prepared," they asserted, "to assent to the terms of the settlement proposed by Virginia." Only a "sincere desire to have harmoniously adjusted all differences" prompted them to "favor the appointment of Commissioners as requested." Suspecting that perhaps the Conference was an attempt to bargain for a peaceful inauguration, as former Governor Chase had suggested, they requested delegates "to use their influence in procuring an adjournment to the fourth day of April next."[14]

Governor Dennison appointed a distinguished delegation: Franklin T. Backus, Salmon P. Chase, Thomas Ewing, William S. Groesbeck, Valentine B. Horton, Reuben Hitchcock, and John C. Wright. All except Groesbeck were Republicans, but opinions ranged from old-line Whiggery to abolitionism. Washington McLean's *Cincinnati Enquirer,* which earlier had urged the Governor to select firm and moderate men, congratulated him on his appointments; but Buckeye radicals were genuinely displeased. Chase particularly was dismayed to find himself the only man "not prepared to go for the Border State Compromise."[15]

Moderate administrations in the Middle Atlantic states, with the enthusiastic support of the financial community, welcomed Virginia's call more sincerely. Governor Morgan sent a special message to the New York Legislature urging participation; Senator Seward endorsed the proposal; and conservatives of all parties joined to pass the enabling resolutions.[16] The Greeleyites of course opposed the invitation, proclaiming it a trap set by slaveholders to ensnare the Republican party.[17] The *Tribune* featured strident editorials under the heading NO MORE COMPROMISES, and a Greeley-inspired minority report found no difference between the proposed meeting at Washington and the secession convention at Montgomery.[18]

Ignoring such hyperbole, a majority in both houses of the New York Legislature voted to send delegates, but specified that acceptance of the invitation was not to be interpreted as an endorsement of the Virginia propositions. After defeating a resolution authorizing the Governor to make the appointments, the two houses finally agreed on a list of eleven delegates representing both the Democratic and Republican parties. When one appointee declined, Weed was nominated in his place; but the Albany editor refused, preferring instead to nominate a representative of the Constitutional Union party. Although the delegation included moderates like William E. Dodge, Erastus Corning, and Francis Granger, Democrats characterized the Republican majority as "a deputation of weak-minded fanatics more fit to represent the whimsies of a Woman's Rights Convention than to confer with statesmen about matters of public moment."[19]

In Pennsylvania, many Republicans demonstrated more concern over passage of the Morrill tariff than over a possible extension of slavery. A farmer from Lancaster County, for example, insisted that wealthy Republican manufacturers preferred to sell iron rather than perpetuate liberty. Republican businessmen in Philadelphia circulated petitions supporting Crittenden's Compromise, and Republican legislators in Harrisburg were "moving in favor of conciliation."[20] Resolutions accepting Virginia's invitation passed by substantial majorities; but, as in New York, the Legislature explicitly indicated that this meant no endorsement for alteration or amendment of the Constitution, such as that suggested in the invitation. All seven delegates appointed by Governor Andrew G. Curtin were Republicans, but a conservative majority favored conciliation. Democrats nevertheless resented particularly the appointment of the notorious radical, David Wilmot; and their state convention censured the Governor for his partisan course in appointing commissioners.[21]

Of all the Northern states, New Jersey probably welcomed Virginia's invitation most enthusiastically. The conservative Republican Governor, Charles S. Olden, promised that the Garden State would make all reasonable and proper concessions to save the Union, and a Democratic majority in the Legislature specifically endorsed Crittenden's Compromise. In the Peace Conference resolutions, members indicated a willingness to support any constitutional method which would permanently settle the question of slavery. Among the highly conciliatory delegation were Governor Olden and his Democratic opponent in 1859, William C. Alexander, a strong Southern rights advocate.[22]

State officials in New England were not disposed to listen sympathetically to Southern appeals for the peaceful salvation of the Union. In fact, every New England state with the exception of Rhode Island displayed a reluctance to accept Virginia's invitation, and eventually delegates were dispatched only because of a desire to provide a Republican majority and to help keep Virginia and

Maryland in the Union until after Lincoln's inauguration.[23] The legislatures of Connecticut, Vermont, and New Hampshire were not in session; and, consequently, Republican governors made the appointments, most of which went to highly partisan irrepressibles. Governor Erastus Fairbanks of Vermont first appointed the state's Congressional delegation, which declined to serve because members did not recognize the authority that called the Conference. The Governor then appointed five stiff-backed citizens and warned them to oppose everything inconsistent with Republican principles.[24] In his instructions to the Connecticut delegation, Governor William A. Buckingham reflected the feelings of most Yankee Republicans when he urged "that no sanction be given to measures which shall bind the government to new guarantees for the protection of property in man."[25]

Conservative forces prevailed in Rhode Island, where Democratic Governor William Sprague, a wealthy cotton mill owner, accepted New York banker August Belmont's conclusion that the popular mind in the North was ready for concession. The Legislature authorized a delegation, and Sprague appointed conciliatory spokesmen. In telegraphing his appointments to Washington, the Governor added fervently, "God give success to the movement."[26]

In Massachusetts, the question of sending delegates aroused animosities among the radicals themselves. While few, if any, Bay State officials were willing to grant concessions, many otherwise uncompromising radicals felt it expedient to answer Virginia's call. A militant group led by Senator Charles Sumner, however, tried desperately to keep the Legislature firm. "If Mass. yields one hairs-breadth," Sumner insisted, "other states will yield an inch, a foot, a furlong." After an excited conversation with Attorney General Edwin M. Stanton, the Senator notified Governor Andrew of a fantastic plot supposedly involving the Conference. According to Sumner's account, Stanton suspected that the Commission was "to contribute a Provisional Govt. which was to take possession of the Capital and declare itself the nation." Congressman Charles Francis Adams analyzed Stanton's fears with less hysteria and gave Andrew rational advice. "If the meeting be a treasonable one," he pointed out, "the Massachusetts delegates would of course be able to expose it to the country. If not, they would appear to take some interest in any proposition to reconcile differences."[27]

Influenced by this reasoning, Governor Andrew reversed himself and supported the dispatch of delegates. "I think we'd better
be present by good men in the Conference," he wrote Sumner,
"than to be misrepresented by volunteers. . . ."[28] Regardless of logic,
Sumner was in no mood to be convinced. In a telegram designed
to block the Governor's proposed course in the Legislature, the
stubborn Senator proclaimed, "I am against sending Commissioners
to treat for the surrender of the North. I stand firm." Andrew
nevertheless commanded a majority, and enabling resolutions
passed after what one inflexible member described as a hard fight
"to keep our good old State up to the mark."[29] Sumner was reassured somewhat when the Governor followed his advice and appointed "only the firmest" Republicans, in whom there was "no
possibility of concession or compromise."[30]

Though convinced of the undesirability of answering Virginia's
"invitation to reverse the verdict of the people," Governor Israel
Washburn of Maine reluctantly followed the lead of Massachusetts.
Motivated solely by the desire to guarantee a Republican majority,
Washburn authorized the Maine Congressional delegation to represent the Pine Tree State. Though this group hardly needed advice
on the dangers of negotiating with slaveholders, they nevertheless
received stern warning: "Artful politicians—rich merchants and
speculators, whose god is money, will counsel peace, regardless
of principal [sic]; see that you yield not to their solicitations."[31]

In another last-minute effort to increase Republican representation, Governor Samuel J. Kirkwood of Iowa adopted Washburn's
expedient and asked the Iowa Congressmen "to attend said meeting on the part of this state if you shall think it advisable to do so
in view of your official positions . . . and of all the surrounding
circumstances."[32]

Unlike the uncompromising Yankees, a majority of border-state
officials accepted Virginia's invitation, though extremist minorities
in some states made serious efforts to send representatives to
Montgomery instead. In Maryland, since the Legislature was not
in session, the decision rested with Governor Thomas Hicks, a
moderate who appointed seven delegates, all devoted Union men.[33]
The Delaware Legislature accepted the invitation almost unanimously and likewise appointed a conservative delegation.[34] Kentucky abandoned its proposal for a border-state convention at

Baltimore, and the Legislature named two Constitutional Unionists, two Breckinridge Democrats, one Douglas Democrat, and one neutral to represent them at Washington. Though the Breckinridge men favored a strong Southern rights position, all agreed with Governor Beriah Magoffin that no experiment should remain untried in restoring fraternal relations.[35]

Tennessee dropped its proposal for a meeting of all the slave-holding states in Nashville, but the state Senate narrowly defeated a proposal by Governor Isham G. Harris and Speaker Tazewell W. Newman to send delegates to Montgomery. Unlike their Governor, however, eleven of the twelve delegates elected by the Legislature stood staunchly for moderation.[36] In North Carolina, Governor John W. Ellis vigorously denounced all "craven Submissionists" and made plans to take the Tar Heel State out of the Union, confidently asserting that the "great heart of the people" would "flock to the Standard of the South." Unionists and Conditional Unionists nevertheless commanded a majority in the Legislature which selected a like-minded delegation to go to Washington. Political necessity, as well as precaution, prompted jittery members to send three observers to Montgomery, also.[37]

Fire-eaters, Black Republicans, and moderates in Missouri clashed in a confusing parliamentary struggle. Governor Claiborne F. Jackson recommended representation at Montgomery, as well as at Washington, but secessionists lacked the strength to force through his recommendation. By voting with radical Republicans from St. Louis County, they managed to postpone a decision; but at last, after three attempts, moderates authorized and elected a delegation, which, like the Legislature itself, was sharply divided, though all members endorsed instructions charging them with the mission of securing the honor and equal rights of the slaveholding states.[38]

When the opening gavel sounded in Washington, legislative battles still continued in Minnesota, Wisconsin, and Michigan, where radicals refused to "yield an inch of . . . vantage ground" after their November victory.[39] *"Southern friends,"* said Governor Alexander Randall of Wisconsin, ". . . have dictated and browbeat long enough."[40] A spirited election to determine whether or not to call a secession convention apparently kept Arkansas from even considering Virginia's invitation. Time and space conspired against the participation of states on the West Coast. No delegates came from the Lower South. The seven seceded states, said the New Orleans *Picayune,* "no longer [had] the capacity to vote as States in the Union."[41] Fire-eaters, like their Northern radical counterparts, feared a negotiated adjustment. Indeed, their success at Montgomery depended upon Virginia's failure at Washington.

## Chapter Five

# A Multitude of Preliminaries

In accordance with Virginia's invitation, some sixty representatives from eleven states assembled at noon on February 4 in Willard's Hall, a reconverted church which the enterprising Willard brothers had incorporated as a part of their hotel. To protect members from intrusion, the city council provided policemen who barred entry from the street and guarded the side entrance to the hotel proper, thereby excluding all visitors. Mayor Berret loaned a fine portrait of General Washington to improve the appearance of the chamber; the city financed a part of the expenses for printing and stationery; and the Willards donated both hall and lights, hoping their use would "be sanctified by restoring peace to the Union." The *Evening Star* thought no place in the city better suited for the purpose, but suggested that portraits of Henry Clay and Andrew Jackson might further enhance the meeting room—ideologically as well as decoratively.[1]

Former Governor Charles S. Morehead of Kentucky called delegates to order for the opening session and nominated Judge John C. Wright as temporary chairman, a proposal adopted unanimously. The Honorable William M. Meredith of Pennsylvania and Governor Chase conducted the aged Ohioan to the chair where he delivered a brief but moving address, pledging a patient and impartial mind and praying for a government more firmly estab-

43

lished than ever before in the affections of his countrymen. Though some listeners had not, as he claimed, assembled "as brothers... animated by the most friendly sentiments," they nevertheless applauded the former Ohio Supreme Court Justice, each interpreting in his own fashion the plea for a Union according to the spirit of the Constitution. "Their appearance," as one member noted, "was grave and their deportment extremely sedate."[2]

When the temporary chairman had concluded, the Conference briefly devoted its energies to initial problems of organization. Benjamin C. Howard of Maryland was unanimously elected temporary secretary; a rules and organization committee of one member from each state, chosen by the respective delegations but appointed by the president, was established with Charles A. Wickliffe as chairman to recommend permanent officers and to report rules of procedure. Since only one-third of the states had as yet responded to Virginia's call, little else could be accomplished. The Conference therefore adjourned to await laggards, some of whom were delayed by the vicissitudes of winter travel, others by recalcitrant legislatures. No one seriously expected representatives from the Lower South, but conservatives still hoped for a pro-compromise reaction that would bring delegates from ultra-Republican states. "The Peace Conference can hardly get fairly to work ere the commencement of next week," reported the *Evening Star* realistically. "There are a multitude of preliminaries to be arranged and disposed of...."[3]

Reassembling at noon on February 5, members authorized a credentials committee, elected permanent officers, and smothered a smoldering controversy over rules. The Vermont delegation registered at Willard's but declined to take seats until additional radical recruits could provide congenial company and greater voting strength. When they put in an appearance next day, bolstered by firm Republicans from Connecticut and Iowa, they complained because "self-appointed managers" had already attended to the work of organization. Delegates had unanimously accepted the selections of the rules and organization committee: John Tyler, president; Crafts J. Wright, secretary.[4]

Upon taking the chair, Tyler delivered an address designed "to draw around Virginia the sympathies of her co-States."[5] Though less than a year earlier he had promised to stand over the graves of his ancestors and defend Southern rights against Republican abolitionists—"live or die, survive or perish," he now spoke in the same magniloquent tones in behalf of "the great work of reconciliation and adjustment."[6] After apologizing for his inadequate command of parliamentary procedure, Tyler quickly roused himself to a florid exhortation which invoked highly sentimental memories of the past. Recalling the similarities between this assemblage and that of "our god-like fathers," the former President challenged delegates to a "task equally grand, equally sublime, quite as full of glory and immortality" as that faced by the Constitutional Convention. "If you reach the height of this great occasion, your children's children will rise up and call you blessed." "To have our names enrolled in the Capitol, to be repeated by future generations with grateful applause—this is an honor higher than the mountains, more enduring than the monumental alabaster." "Your patriotism," he concluded with unwarranted assurance, "will surmount the difficulties, however great, if you will but accomplish one triumph in advance, and that is, a triumph over *party*."[7]

Though few of the delegates, perhaps least of all President Tyler himself, had any intention of triumphing over their respective parties, listeners were nevertheless impressed by his address—the principal business of the second day. One distinguished delegate described it as electrical in effect; others declared their readiness to unite with Virginia in any measures of conciliation. Although denied entry to the hall, newspaper correspondents found no difficulty in assessing reactions. A "beautiful and touching production, though entirely *extempore*," reported the *Missouri Republican;* "one of the most affecting and eloquent efforts . . . ever spoken in this country," said the *Evening Star;* its "highly patriotic and conciliatory" character had "the happiest effect on the Convention," concluded the *New York Times*.[8] Former Speaker of the House Robert C. Winthrop of Massachusetts lauded it as a felicitous utterance which he hoped might actuate all the proceedings. Even the uncompromising Samuel Ryan Curtis called it an apppropriate speech.[9]

Identifying partisanship with Republicanism, border-state moderates reiterated Tyler's appeal with the naïve hope of persuading Northern radicals to compromise. "I came here to act for the Union—the whole Union," declared Governor Morehead of Kentucky. "I recognize no sides—no party." Reverdy Johnson of Maryland inveighed against use of the word *party,* and Judge Ruffin of North Carolina ingenuously urged members to discard politics and be brethren and friends.[10] Reuben Hitchcock, an Ohio Republican who favored the "true Hickory ring of the Chicago platform," admitted that there was "too general a feeling that party is paramount to the Union." "I fear that ... the apprehension of injuring the [Republican] party will lead to a policy which will destroy both it & the country."[11] In spite of partisanship, however, there remained a hope that through face-to-face discussion "the disputes which now disturb the country ... might be amicably settled ... without loss of honour on either side."[12]

For fear members might weaken in the face of persuasion, various state legislatures had precautionary restrictions inserted in the enabling resolutions. Delegates from Indiana, Illinois, New York, Pennsylvania, Massachusetts, Missouri, and Virginia were specifically subject to legislative control. The legislatures of Ohio, Indiana, Illinois, and New York indicated an unwillingness to entertain Virginia's proposed adjustment. Those of Ohio and Illinois urged a postponement of proceedings in accordance with Chase's slogan: "Inauguration first—adjustment afterwards." The Pennsylvania resolution indicated that the people of that state wanted no alteration of the Constitution. Tennessee threatened to sever all connections with states refusing reasonable guarantees for the state's future safety. Delaware expected its delegates to emulate the example of "the immortal patriots who framed the Federal Constitution, by sacrificing all minor considerations upon the altar of the Union."[13]

Those who wanted the Conference to succeed thus compared it with that of the founding fathers and urged delegates to adopt the rules of the Constitutional Convention. Northern radicals, on the other hand, looked upon it as an illegal or certainly as an extra-legal gathering. Amos Tuck of New Hampshire called it "a body unknown to the Constitution and the laws"; Curtis, "a kind of semi official legislative body"; John G. Nicolay and John Hay, "an assembly, somewhat anomalous in character and authority"; David Dudley Field of New York, "an irregular body sitting by the side of a legislative body ... attempting to influence its action." "Although I do not regard this Conference as exactly

unconstitutional," said Field, "it is certainly a bad precedent."
Roger Baldwin, leader of the Connecticut delegation, thought it
"a *revolutionary proceeding*" without "sufficient cause or justification."[14] Radical editors dramatized this view for their Northern
readers. Taking its cue from Field's friend, Horace Greeley, the
*Kennebec Journal* compared it to the meeting of Benedict Arnold
and Major André.[15]

Moderates quite logically complained that such accusations
brought the Union another step toward dissolution. James Guthrie
of Kentucky replied to Baldwin's charge by asserting the right of
petition. "It is all legitimate," he insisted, "and legitimate in the
most technical sense."[16]

The rules adopted on the third day, February 6, reflected the
attitudes of the conservatives, who proudly proclaimed them substantially those of the Constitutional Convention. Radicals particularly objected to the secrecy rule designed to encourage delegates
to talk to *each other* rather than to the newspapers. Controversy
over this point began the first day when reporters were excluded
by a voice vote and continued intermittently until February 15 when
"distorted and perverted" newspaper accounts prompted a reconsideration which failed. Some radical delegates even advocated
admitting the public, a suggestion opposed by a large majority.
Citing the Constitutional Conventon as a model, Wickliffe declared
secrecy absolutely indispensable to successful action, since publicity
would render any change of policy difficult, if not impossible. "I
wish to have our time used in consultation and in action," he concluded, "not consumed in political speech-making." "Every one,"
Seddon agreed, "should be left free to make ... concessions, and
not subject himself to unfavorable public criticism by doing so."[17]

Though it excluded their correspondents, conservative papers
nevertheless favored secrecy. The editor of the *Evening Star* saw
no reason to regret the decision to consult and confer like members of one household "rather than as partisan politicians striving
to make political capital for sectional or party advantage." "This
[rule]," said the outspoken Sam Medary of the procompromise
Columbus, Ohio, *Crisis*, "has given mortal offence to that class of
editors who live by excitement and sensation." Delegates, he
thought, should meet in the most free and easy manner—a pose
which might be "easily misconstrued and sent over the country

to do much mischief."[18] Editors thus interpreted continuation of the secrecy rule as a victory for those who placed their faith in frank and full discussion—uninfluenced and uninhibited by the presence of the press.

Closely linked with the controversy over secrecy was that over keeping a record of proceedings. The Conference first authorized two, and later four, assistant secretaries, none of whom were delegates: William W. Hoppin of Rhode Island, J. Henry Puleston of Pennsylvania, John Stryker of New York, and James M. Tower of New Jersey. This staff, headed by Crafts J. Wright, kept an official journal which only members could inspect. No copy of a journal entry was permitted without specific Conference authorization during the sitting of the Convention. In addition, Lucius E. Chittenden kept an unofficial record based upon as full and accurate notes as his strength would permit. "I have endeavored to follow . . . the example of the illustrious Reporter of the Constitutional Convention . . .," he explained, "and while my notes lack the beauty and felicity which characterize his, I trust they are not less full and accurate." Several determined Republican efforts to secure a stenographic account of the debates ended in defeat, thanks to the opposition of every Southern state.[19] As a result, the official record was, as Wright admitted, full of errors.[20]

The eighteen rules initially adopted included trivial, incidental, and ambiguous provisions, as well as some significant omissions or deliberate oversights. Since state representation varied haphazardly from three to twelve members, voting necessarily had to be by states, with seven delegations designated as a quorum. At first, record was kept of only the decision by states, though provision was made later for members to enter a dissent. No one could speak oftener than twice without special leave on the same question, and not a second time until all others had been heard. At adjournment no one was to leave his place "until the President pass." No appeal was provided from a decision of the chair, a mistake remedied later. Some rules, particularly the one on secrecy, needed clarification; and even when clarified, they were apparently ignored. Though obviously all contingencies had not been anticipated, no governing body of parliamentary procedure was specified.[21]

During the course of the Conference, several lively arguments developed over attempts to limit debate, a restriction no doubt deliberately omitted from the initial rules. As March 4 approached, procompromise delegates became increasingly annoyed at the Republican strategy of delay. "Our true policy," said J. Z. Goodrich, an uncompromising Massachusetts delegate, "is to delay matters—finally do nothing, relying on Providence and honest 'Old Abe' to work out the problem of American destiny...."[22] In pursuing this policy, radicals strenuously opposed efforts to limit debate, despite fervent pleas from border-state moderates who warned that adjournment of Congress would make subsequent action futile. A chaotic discussion prompted by a motion to limit each speaker to thirty minutes (later amended to ten minutes) consumed almost an entire day. Since little of the commentary pertained to the subject at issue, Reuben Hitchcock eventually rose to make the appropriate point of order. "The gentleman is undoubtedly correct...," President Tyler observed despairingly, "but the discussion of the general subject has been permitted to go on without objection by the Convention, and I do not think it would be right to stop it now." When put to a vote, the motion to limit debate failed, with every Northern state except New Jersey and Rhode Island opposing it.[23] Later, Wickliffe led a successful attempt to curb discussion on amendments, but the large delegation of uncompromising Republicans made prolonged sessions inevitable. "They can," said Doniphan, "babble us to all eternity."[24]

Former Secretary of the Treasury James Guthrie of Kentucky proposed the most important item of procedure, a committee of one from each state with the responsibility of considering all resolutions and reporting those deemed "right, necessary, and proper to restore harmony and preserve the Union." Seddon vigorously opposed this suggestion as contrary to the instructions of the Virginia Legislature, which of course had specified a basis of adjustment. With some logic, Seddon contended that shifting responsibility to a committee merely delayed consideration by the entire membership—a group "not in itself too large for convenient deliberation." Ignoring Seddon's objections, the Conference adopted Guthrie's proposal without division. To hasten the report scheduled for February 8, the committee met during Conference sessions with Guthrie as chairman and Puleston as secretary.[25] Each representative was elected by his state delegation and appointed by President Tyler: New Hampshire, Asa Fowler; Vermont, Hiland Hall; Rhode Island, Samuel Ames; Connecticut, Roger S. Baldwin;

New Jersey, Joseph F. Randolph; Pennsylvania, Thomas White; Delaware, Daniel M. Bates; North Carolina, Thomas Ruffin; Kentucky, James Guthrie; Ohio, Thomas Ewing; Indiana, Caleb B. Smith; Illinois, Stephen T. Logan; Iowa, James Harlan; Maryland, Reverdy Johnson; Virginia, James A. Seddon; New York, David Dudley Field; Missouri, Alexander W. Doniphan; Tennessee, Felix K. Zollicoffer; Maine, Lot M. Morrill; Massachusetts, Francis B. Crowninshield.[26] Radicals who originally welcomed the committee as a means of delay were unhappy later because its members did not, in their opinion, represent the Convention fairly.[27]

Outnumbered fourteen states to seven, Southern representatives, as Reverdy Johnson recalled, implored their Northern brethren to agree to something that might satisfy the South, but earnest discussion met the stern opposition of uncompromising Yankees, particularly Field, Baldwin, and Crowninshield.[28] "Crowninshield is a trump on the Committee," Goodrich exclaimed in a report to Governor Andrew, "& all my troops . . . behave admirably."[29]

From February 6 to February 15, the committee sat while the Conference waited. On February 8, the day scheduled for a report, Guthrie requested further time, promising action as soon as "a proper regard to the interests of all sections will permit." A motion by James B. Clay of Kentucky to extend the time to February 11 passed without division, but when that day came Guthrie found it necessary to ask for another postponement. On February 13, he again repeated his request. "The Committee on Resolutions, &c., have labored diligently and held protracted sessions," he said; but no report could be made despite the "necessity for immediate action."[30] With some justification, Goodrich boasted to Andrew of the successful radical strategy: "[Guthrie's request] was at once granted, with the hearty thanks of us northern *radicals*. . . . It puts us 2 days nearer to the 4th of March."[31]

After a prolonged session "until a late hour" on February 14, the committee by a bare majority passed a compromise proposal which Guthrie presented to the Conference next morning. Since Secretary Puleston's notes were not available to reporters, newspapers could only speculate upon the vote and the secret committee proceedings.[32] With the report at last before the entire delegation, John M. Forbes noted "a good spirit here . . . but we have only just began [*sic*] to skirmish as yet. . . ."[33]

## Chapter Six

# Masterly Inactivity

Good nature & masterly inactivity," said a member of the Massachusetts delegation, "is the policy till Lincoln is inaugurated."[1] Lincoln and Vice-President-elect Hannibal Hamlin had reportedly agreed on such a program at their meeting in Chicago late in November, and Republican Congressmen endorsed it at a caucus in Washington on December 3.[2] "If the South is let alone," Republicans argued, "its own disagreements will soon block the operations of the fire eaters."[3] Carl Schurz urged Congressmen to "discuss every proposition at length, make speech upon speech, motion upon motion."[4] Even the excitable Greeley advised his followers to talk smoothly until "in a position to *use* daggers as well as speak them."[5] Radicals on the Guthrie Committee thus followed an accepted Congressional policy of calculated delay, a policy which gave Republicans time to rally Northern opinion, as well as time for Southern passions to cool. Then, if worst came to worst, it placed secessionists in the awkward position of having to make the first belligerent move.

Continued negotiations at the Peace Conference likewise helped to keep the border states in the Union, thereby insuring a quorum in Congress for counting the electoral vote and Lincoln's subsequent inauguration.[6] As one radical phrased it, "It is probable

51

that the Peace Congress ... will carry us over a good many days and aid to bring the 4th of March innocuous."[7] John A. Gilmer of North Carolina pointed out the obvious strategic advantage in thus isolating the cotton states. "If the Republicans will confer & work daily ... ," he advised Thurlow Weed, "they can without yielding ... save Del. M$^{d}$ Va. N.C. Ky. Tenn. Mo. and perhaps Louisiana & Texas. ..." Impressed by this advice, the eminently practical Weed assured Lincoln that the government could not "obtain money to war with the whole South." "If all those states go out," he said, "the Capitalists, Merchants, &c &c will say 'let them alone.' "[8]

In Washington, Weed's close associate, Senator Seward, worked to "gain time for the new administration to organize." When a radical delegate threatened to disrupt Peace Conference proceedings with "a vigorous and warning speech," Seward apprised him of an editorial from the *Richmond Enquirer* accusing the incoming Secretary of State of pursuing a policy designed to get Lincoln "firmly settled in power."[9]

By temporizing, conservative Republicans like Weed and Seward risked losing both the border states and the radical wing of their party. Border-state secessionists immediately identified so obvious a strategy. "The Abolitionists will continue to amuse us with hopes of Compromise without any real purpose to make a Substantial Settlement," said Governor John W. Ellis of North Carolina. "They are Seeking time within which to get control of the army and navy and the power of the government."[10] Just before the North Carolina election, Peace Conference delegate Daniel M. Barringer telegraphed: "Delay is a part of their game."[11] Secessionist sympathizers in Virginia heralded Seward's duplicity and stirred up excitement and alarm designed to hasten disunion.[12] In Missouri, Governor Jackson declared that honor, interests, and sympathy pointed alike in one direction: *"to stand by the South."*[13]

Worse, perhaps, than failure to hold the border states, Republicans feared disrupting the party "by some shabby compromise."[14] Radicals such as Oliver P. Morton, Carl Schurz, David Dudley Field, Lyman Trumbull, Elihu B. Washburne, Salmon P. Chase, and Mongomery Blair warned each other and anyone else who would listen of this imminent danger.[15] Ultra-radicals like Charles Sumner and Joshua R. Giddings accused Seward of attempting to "disband our organization." "... [M]en are ready to fight," said Giddings, "but not to compromise."[16] Greeley's Washington correspondent talked of attempts to "defraud the party of the legitimate results of its victory," and the *Tribune* predicted disaster in the spring elections unless compromise overtures were promptly arrested and repudiated.[17] Both conservatives and radicals communicated their contradictory fears to Lincoln. "If you waver," Washburne counseled, *"our party has gone."*[18] Intraparty strife and indecision, as well as deliberate policy, thus promoted delay.

Some delegates found Washington a congenial place to pass the time while awaiting the Guthrie Committee report; others came with dual purposes which could be profitably pursued while the Conference waited. Most conspicuous among this latter group was the presiding officer himself, who served not only as a delegate but as Virginia's commissioner to President Buchanan. The Virginia resolutions provided that Tyler request the President to abstain "from any and all acts calculated to produce a collision of arms" during the Conference. Judge John Robertson went on a similar mission to the seceded states, where he failed to obtain the requested pledges but nevertheless succeeded in intensifying the campaign to bring Virginia into the Confederacy.[19]

In spite of "severe indisposition" and "every possible personal inconvenience," Tyler had left the comforts of Sherwood Forest on January 22 to confer with Governor Letcher on his double mission. Next morning, he took the train for Washington and immediately on his arrival he asked for an audience with Buchanan, who received him cordially on January 24, but made no promise, pleading that "the whole power rested with Congress." "His policy," Tyler reported, "obviously is to throw all responsibility off his shoulders."[20] In a special message to Congress on January 28, however, the cautious Commander in Chief presented Tyler's proposal with a request to refrain "from passing any law calculated to produce a collision." The Republican majority ignored his plea, refusing even to refer the Virginia resolutions to a committee.[21]

Meanwhile, Tyler investigated federal military and naval operations. He discovered that the steamship *Brooklyn* had sailed for the South with troops shortly before his arrival. President Buchanan promptly assured him that the vessel was not destined to South Carolina, but to Fort Pickens at Pensacola on an errand of "mercy and relief."[22] Fearful that the expedition might nevertheless incite some hostile act, the Secretaries of War and Navy ordered the commander not to land unless the fort was attacked.[23] General Scott's "absurd and high-handed course" in arming the capital prompted Tyler to consider, for a time at least, requesting Governor Letcher to muster 5,000 Old Dominion troops at Alexandria to counteract those of the federal government. The ubiquitous commissioner also became agitated over a rumor that cannon at Fortress Monroe had been turned landward toward Virginia, a charge never substantiated, but one which the President, at Tyler's request, dutifully ordered the Secretary of War to investigate.[24]

Displaying an unprecedented deference to the aging ex-President, Buchanan called on Tyler at his suite at Brown's Hotel, a visit which the socially ambitious Mrs. Tyler supposed was his first "since being the nation's chief." When General Scott scheduled a parade of federal troops on Washington's Birthday, the President paid Tyler a second call to make sure the display would not offend "the susceptibilities of members of the Peace Convention." Since Tyler of course assured him it would, Buchanan made a last-minute attempt to cancel the performance and then reversed his decision in order to avoid "giving serious offense to the tens of thousands of people" who had assembled to see it.[25]

The President's deference enhanced Tyler's effectiveness as an intermediary for Judge Robertson and secessionist leaders, including Governor Francis Pickens of South Carolina. But Republicans, naturally enough, became alarmed by the negotiations of a Peace Conference official who doubled as Virginia's agent in treating with secessionists. "This activity in behalf of insurgents and traitors," said the *New York Times,* "could not fail to neutralize the apparent zeal of the ex-President for peace." "Don't trust him," warned Sumner, always eager to believe the worst; "he means to betray you."[26]

In quarters with his wife and his two youngest children at Brown's, the former President surrounded himself with devoted admirers. A fellow delegate from Virginia valued his influence in advance of all others, but the *Evening Star* charged that he fell wholly into the hands of the malevolent Senator Louis T. Wigfall of Texas, "whom he really represented." A levee of distinguished personalities crowded his private parlor, and some were amazed to find him unchanged in energy of body and mind "even under the weight of so many years." Correspondence from every quarter cluttered his writing table, and a roster of members with penciled notations indicating hotel room numbers testified to his diligent activity. Though fatigued and forced to resort to sedatives, he nevertheless looked remarkably well, according to his admiring wife, who thought him to be "in a stronger condition to bear up than for many a day." On the eve of his labors, he "retired upon a dose of hydrargum," thereby making ready "to snatch from ruin a great and glorious confederation."[27]

Like Tyler, many Northern delegates came to Washington with dual purposes. The Massachusetts delegation put aside its peaceful mission and called on General Scott to discuss the tender of volunteers.[28] John M. Forbes delayed his appearance at Willard's in order to help Governor Andrew plan the logistics of moving Bay State troops to Washington. One evening soon after his arrival, the Massachusetts railroad promoter labored until past midnight with Lieutenant Gustavus V. Fox and General Scott devising strategy for the relief of Fort Sumter.[29] Vermont's Lucius E. Chittenden called at Winder's Building to question Scott about military precautions. The impressive General "raised his gigantic frame" from the sofa on which he was reclining to advise the inquisitive radical that he was alert to the danger of revolution. "The Vermont delegation," Chittenden replied, "will sleep more quietly tonight. . . ." Reassured about the safety of Washington, Chittenden took a train one Sunday for Baltimore where his amateur detective work confirmed rumors of a plot to assassinate Lincoln.[30] General John E. Wool, a New York delegate, continued to perform his duties as Commander of the Eastern Department of the Army, a unit embracing the Southern seaboard. ". . . I am prepared against all threats," he assured Lincoln, "to see you safely placed in the Presidential chair."[31]

Since Congressional delegations represented Maine and Iowa, members necessarily had to choose how to divide their time between the two bodies. Five of the seven members from Maine decided to devote their energies to Congress, leaving Daniel E. Somes and Lot M. Morrill to represent the Pine Tree State in Peace Conference deliberations. Senator Fessenden explained his absence on the ground that no good results could come from such a gathering.[32] Senator James W. Grimes of Iowa expressed a similar conviction and rarely, if ever, attended, thus relinquishing the responsibility to Senator James Harlan and Representatives Samuel Ryan Curtis and William Vandever.[33] Dividing his attention between negotiating for peace and preparing for war, Curtis presented to the House Military Committee a bill designed to strengthen presidential control of state militia and to give the President power to call out volunteers.[34]

Delegates also devoted time to various business and political enterprises. James Guthrie worried about the problems of secession as they related to his Louisville and Nashville Railroad, including the need for additional compensation from the Post Office Department to cover the heavy increase in mail.[35] In Congress on February 20, Curtis, Fessenden, Morrill, and others successfully negotiated a tariff increase, thereby raising a formidable economic barrier to peaceful adjustment while redeeming a Republican promise.[36] Curtis and Forbes, particularly, worked diligently for the passage of a transcontinental railroad bill.[37] "My great effort...has been to get through the Pacific Railroad," Curtis confessed to his diary; later, he told his wife that "business in the House prevents me from doing much at the Convention."[38]

In an effort to encourage conciliation, leading New York bankers and Wall Street brokers warned Frederick T. Frelinghuysen of New Jersey that they would not advance one cent to the incoming administration unless some adjustment were arrived at. Reacting negatively to this kind of pressure, Republican delegates Cook, Palmer, and Wood telegraphed Governor Yates urging Illinois to guarantee her proportion of the government loan, thereby counteracting Eastern financial influence.[39]

Southern delegates were subject to economic pressures designed to strengthen border-state securities. Noting that prices "will undoubtedly advance in view of a settlement or of the *probability* of one," Ward and Company of New York urged Judge Ruffin to "advise whether we shall purchase or wait." After generously offering to bear a part of Ruffin's expenses, another correspondent begged: "Do not plunge us into a state of anarchy without any warning. Give the business community time to arrange for the crops...."[40]

Republican delegates neglected their Conference duties to squabble with one another over patronage. General Doniphan estimated that "at least fifty open and avowed office seekers" had "availed themselves of the opportunity of visiting Washington at the expense of their respective states & haveing [*sic*] at the same time some decent pretext for being here, so as not to seem to be mere cormorants & birds of prey."[41] Curtis complained that his correspondence was "mostly about office"; the *New York Times* noted the pressure of job applicants on Conference members; and Shillington's Bookstore disposed of nearly the entire edition of *A Guide to Office Seekers,* which provided a list of all government offices and salaries.[42]

Doniphan's estimate was hardly an exaggeration.* Chase, Smith, Tuck, Field, Wilmot, and Curtis had been mentioned as Cabinet possibilities, and many aspired to lesser stations.[43] Those who were not themselves candidates had friends to support. As Hoosier delegate Godlove Orth frankly confessed, "... it may be pleasant at least, if not profitable to have a friend 'near the throne'...."[44] In suggesting Massachusetts delegate Theophilus P. Chandler for postmaster of Boston, Governor Andrew advised boldness in managing the patronage. "We must *use* power, when we have it," he said. Goodrich, needing no such obvious advice, interviewed Lincoln "3 or 4 times" in behalf of various candidates, once marshaling the entire Massachusetts delegation to urge Chase for the Treasury.[45] James Pollock and William McKennan, Pennsylvania delegates, supported Simon Cameron for this job, while Grimes and Fessenden took special pains to oppose the conservative Pennsylvanian. Chase himself warned Lincoln against Caleb B. Smith.[46]

No office was seemingly too obscure to invite rivalry. When delegate Thomas Turner took an interest in the Illinois marshal's job, a rival candidate in the state Legislature complained to his Congressman. Burton C. Cook and John Wood of the same delegation had a candidate for commissioner to the Sandwich Islands, and Cook's brother-in-law sought an appointment in the New York customs

* Chase became Secretary of the Treasury; Smith, Secretary of the Interior. James Pollock became Director of the Philadelphia Mint; J. Z. Goodrich, Collector of Customs in Boston; L. E. Chittenden, Register of the Treasury; Ezra B. French, Second Auditor of the Treasury. Tuck was appointed Naval Officer of the Port of Boston, where "the salary was good, the duties light and the dignity all that could be desired."—Charles R. Corning, *Amos Tuck* (Exeter, N.H., n.d.), p. 90.

house.[47] Illinois members seemingly had an advantage, and Fessenden became "pained and disgusted with the ill-bred, ravenous crowd" that surrounded the President-elect. "Everything in the way of office goes West," he complained. "We shall hardly get the pairings [*sic*] of a toenail in New England."[48]

When not engrossed in business deals or patronage squabbles delegates found time to pursue their own fancies. Christopher P. Wolcott and David Dudley Field tried cases before the Supreme Court, while Franklin T. Backus, Burton C. Cook, Reuben Hitchcock, John M. Palmer, Thomas J. Turner, and Levi Underwood arranged to be admitted to practice before the country's highest tribunal. Others accepted Mathew B. Brady's generous invitation to sit for photographs. Many no doubt availed themselves of admission cards provided by the doorkeeper of the House of Representatives. Chittenden, for example, negotiated the length of Pennsylvania Avenue to observe the counting of the electoral vote on February 13. Palmer became bored with the parade of notables. "You get tired of looking at distinguished men," he confided to his wife, "for after all there is no great difference between men."[49]

Early in the Conference, members called in a body on President Buchanan, who looked careworn but received the group cordially. In shaking hands, he begged each delegate to save the country from "bloody, fratricidal war." These "puling entreaties" so annoyed one radical Vermonter that six years later he recalled the incident with revulsion. Buchanan entertained the resolutions committee at a dinner on the day of its report, and Secretary of War Joseph Holt held a supper for the same group late that same evening. Some members necessarily declined because of illness. During their three-week sojourn in Washington, Tyler, Wool, Johnson, Doniphan, and Rives suffered maladies variously described as "inflammation of the lungs," "sickness," and "pneumonia."[50]

The socially inclined crowded into the home of Senator and Mrs. Stephen A. Douglas on the evening of February 12 for what was described as a grand party, including some four hundred "Senators Representatives generals members of the Peace Conference Vice President Tyler and his wife." "Mrs. Douglas is a fine woman," said one captivated guest, "and plays the agreeable hostess in admirable style...."[51]

Charlotte Cushman, the celebrated actress, nightly attracted an "immense, intense jam" at the Eleventh Street Theatre. "No such furore has been exhibited among play-goers here for years," said the *Evening Star*. "A large number of the leading members of Congress, and other prominent personages" petitioned her to do *Hamlet*. Editorials discussed her "superb *physique*," but Palmer wrote his wife of "a very coarse performance." Some Old Gentlemen apparently whiled away time by observing worldly affairs transacted in crowded lobbies; in any event, one Illinois rustic scrutinized rather carefully "the wretched heartless life of the Belles that really infest the hotels."[52]

While delegates thus amused themselves, several anxious assemblies awaited word from Willard's for signs of conciliation or conflict. At the other end of Pennsylvania Avenue, Representative Thomas Corwin, chairman of the House Committee of Thirty-three, postponed his proposed compromise report in the hope that the Peace Congress might present a more acceptable substitute. Most Republican Congressmen, however, bent their energies to defeat all such proposals in both assemblies. The day the Conference convened, Representative John F. Potter of Wisconsin called a meeting to rally the forty to fifty "regular, straight-out no compromise men" in Congress.[53] Governor Andrew urged Massachusetts members to "surround our Commissioners with the best influences," particularly with radicals like Montgomery Blair and Fessenden.[54] On February 7, New York delegate James Wadsworth assembled those commissioners who might be absolutely relied upon, and at least three such gatherings of firm ones met during the course of the Conference with Chase as chairman. Although attendance was not as large as expected, participants agreed to delay all action until it had first been considered in caucus.[55]

At the provisional seat of Secessia in Montgomery, fire-eaters likewise attempted to thwart all attempts at adjustment. Officials of the provisional government telegraphed sympathetic border-state members urging them not to consent to compromise of any kind. *"The only hope now,"* concluded a correspondent for the Charleston *Mercury*, *"is in the smashing up of the Peace Congress and getting Virginia out."*[56]

More moderate Southerners sent messages indicating a continued interest in the reconstruction of the Union. Tyler, for example, received "a most important dispatch" from Montgomery

announcing that the Convention there awaited the result of the
Peace Conference; but regardless of such assurances, the inauguration of Jefferson Davis proceeded, as scheduled, on February 18.[57]
"Overtures of reconciliation will have no influence in staying the
action of the Convention," said the *New York Times* correspondent in Montgomery, "but they do and *will* have great weight with
the people."[58]

The Virginia Convention assembled at Richmond on February
13, and members of the moderate majority hoped daily for an
acceptable Peace Conference report. After noting "the ability, patriotism & good feelings" of some of his fellow commissioners,
William C. Rives sent word from Washington which encouraged
hope. "With so little to settle," said Rives' brother, Alexander, a
member of the Virginia Senate, "it is scarcely credible that such
men, as ... Guthrie, Ewing, Ruffin of N.C. &c. &c. cannot bring
about a harmonious result." After the annoying ten-day delay,
however, the Virginia Senator displayed less confidence. "We are
all anxiety here about the result of your labors in the Conference,"
he wrote. "Many prayers are put up by the disunionists for its
failure, but as we are told 'the prayers of the wicked avail nought'
we are not discouraged. The salvation of the Country depends on
your success."[59] George W. Summers, who had left Washington to
take his seat in the Virginia Convention, received letters warning
that "every hour of *delay* ... was an hour of *danger*."[60]

Tyler, who like Summers had been elected to the Virginia Convention, advised his fellow Virginians to adjourn from day to day
until some decision was reached in Washington. Impatient to take
his seat in Richmond, he frequently threatened that "unless something was done" Virginia would "retire with dignity from the field
to join without loss of time her more Southern sisters." Such action, Tyler felt, would confront the Lincoln administration with an
"array of power" sufficient to "force the northern people to a reconstruction of the Union as in 1787."[61]

On February 13, the death of Judge Wright, the temporary
chairman, caused an unforeseen delay in Conference proceedings.
"His sudden death in the midst of our deliberations," said Rives,
"seems to me to exalt—in some degree to canonize—our labors."
Some members indeed saw "a manifestation of the visible hand of
God" in the "solemn responsibilities of the Conference." At a spe-

cial session on February 14, Chase, Wickliffe, Loomis, Ewing, and Rives delivered highly sentimental eulogies, and the Reverend Charles H. Hall read the service of the Episcopal Church. The funeral cortege then proceeded from Willard's to the Baltimore and Ohio station. Crafts Wright returned his father's body to Cincinnati, while J. Henry Puleston acted as secretary in his absence. At the suggestion of Chase, Governor Dennison replaced the moderate Mr. Wright with Christopher P. Wolcott of Akron, a militant radical.[62] The *Cincinnati Enquirer* lauded Wright's noble mission and deplored Wolcott's appointment as a serious threat to a liberal adjustment.[63] Despite his effusive eulogy mingling private with public grief, Chase welcomed the depletion of conservative strength in the Ohio delegation. "Among so many *very old gentlemen*," said one of his correspondents, "such an *actuary* as Mr. Wright would tell us, the chances are that every sixty days will improve the *quality* of the convention."[64]

## Chapter Seven

# The Rhetoric of Compromise and Conflict

On February 15, after eleven days of delay, the Guthrie Committee presented a majority report and two dissenting alternatives. Although less acceptable than the Crittenden Compromise to most Southern delegates, the majority resolutions followed Crittenden's formula in recommending seven articles for a proposed Thirteenth Amendment to the Constitution. Border-state moderates like Rives, for example, felt that "everything of substance" was "unequivocally secured": (1) involuntary service was to be protected in the territories south of the Missouri Compromise line and prohibited north of it; (2) territory was not to be acquired without ratification by four-fifths of the Senate; (3) Congress was not to interfere with slavery in the city of Washington without the consent of Maryland, and it was not to have power to regulate, abolish, or control slavery in states where it existed; (4) the fugitive slave law was to be enforced; (5) the importation of slaves was to be forever prohibited; (6) the first, second, third, and fifth provisions, and specified articles in the Constitution relating to slavery were not to be amended or abolished without the consent of all the states; (7) slaveholders were to be compensated for fugitives lost through violence or intimidation.*

Extremists of both sides denounced the majority proposals. Ardent defenders of Southern rights dismissed them as "wishy-washy resolutions, that amount to nothing." Ultra-Republicans, of course, repudiated them as a total surrender of principles, and endorsed the minority report of Roger Baldwin calling for a national convention as originally suggested by Kentucky.[1] Radicals enthusiastically supported this alternative because it insured delay without forfeiting any of the provisions of their Chicago platform, particularly SECTION 8 denying the authority of Congress "or of any individuals, to give legal existence to Slavery in any Territory of the United States."[2] Guthrie called Baldwin's alternative a new excuse for inaction and urged delegates to act first upon the majority report. "If we adopt the gentleman's views, go home and do nothing," Guthrie warned, "we take the responsibility of breaking up the Government."[3]

On behalf of the opposite minority, James A. Seddon reintroduced as a substitute the resolutions of the Virginia General Assembly with certain alternatives of his own designed to alter drastically the federal system of constitutional government. In order to guarantee Southern rights, Seddon proposed what was in effect a Southern veto on both legislation and executive appointments. In addition, persons of the African race were prohibited from voting or holding office, and states were explicitly granted the right to *dissolve* their relationship with the federal government and withdraw from the Union.[4]

Six days of parliamentary chaos followed the introduction of these three reports. Although President Tyler ruled that the first question would be the substitution of the Baldwin report for that of the majority, delegates failed to limit themselves to this issue, but

---

* Rives makes an extensive comparison of the Peace Conference Resolutions and the Crittenden Compromise in William C. Rives, *Speech of Hon. William C. Rives on the Proceedings of the Peace Conference and the State of the Union, delivered in Richmond, Virginia, March 8, 1861* (Richmond, 1861), 3 ff. Crittenden's proposals specifically "recognized" and "protected as property" "slavery of the African race" in territory "now held or hereafter acquired" south of 36° 30'; they permitted territories both north and south of that line to enter the Union "with or without slavery"; and there was to be no abolition of slavery in the District of Columbia without the consent of Virginia as well as Maryland.—*Cong. Globe,* 36 Cong., 2 sess., 112–14; Chittenden, *Report,* 43–45.

instead talked about those features of the crisis which concerned them.[5] In the confusion, everyone apparently forgot Tyler's initial ruling. Amendments were appended to amendments and substitutions substituted for substitutions. Sessions were prolonged, laborious and exciting; and with considerable justification James B. Clay compared proceedings to the "circumlocution office" in Dickens' *Bleak House*.[6]

Ninety-one of the delegates made statements which Chittenden recorded with questionable accuracy in a *Report* published three years later.[7] Committee chairman James Guthrie spoke some sixty-one times in favor of the majority proposal. The cadaverous Mr. Seddon argued militantly for Southern rights on fifty-three different occasions. Charles A. Wickliffe spoke fifty-one times; and Thomas Ewing, Sr., an unusually effective conciliator, twenty times. Those described as ultra-Black Republicans were comparatively less vocal. David Dudley Field, characterized as a weak-minded fanatic by the Albany *Atlas and Argus,* led the anticompromise delegation with twenty-nine pronouncements, followed by former Governor Chase with twenty-eight and David Wilmot with twenty.[8]

Impressed by the grave constitutional crisis, delegates took themselves and their mission very seriously, often asserting that they spoke for their respective states, sections, or economic groups. William C. Noyes, for example, claimed to speak for New York, Boutwell for Massachusetts, Barringer for North Carolina—if not the whole South—and Dodge for the commercial interests.[9] In a bitter exchange with Granger over who properly represented Northern opinion, Noyes announced: "Sir, I speak for New York! ... Not New York of an old fossiliferous era ... but young, breathing, living New York, as she exists today." Speakers sometimes used public opinion as a persuasive weapon, claiming that those whom they represented insisted upon a prescribed course of action. "Unless you use language and adopt terms ... which will satisfy the seceded States," said Barringer, "... your labors will have been in vain." Stockton asserted that Northern moderates would resist coercion—a remark denounced by the *New York Tribune* as treasonable.[10]

Members were quick to sense personal or sectional affront; some were pompous and austere; many were highly sentimental. Although much of their language might well have been taken from currently popular melodrama, apparently it prompted no offense.

At least there was no cynical amusement from such a line as, "Little Rhode Island has a heart which beats true to the Union." Chittenden recorded little if any humor, a reflection not only of his own stern outlook, but no doubt also that of his colleagues. Reverdy Johnson once made a heavy-handed reference intended as humor, but no humorous response was recorded. "I won't dispute about terms," he told Seddon. "In all such discussions, Heaven save me from a Virginia politician."[11]

Speeches were "earnest, sometimes exciting, but generally conciliatory."[12] Despite a number of sharp interchanges, most delegates reported a general atmosphere of amicability. Baldwin recalled "a pervading spirit of courtesy and conciliation,"[13] while Summers limited this "growing spirit of brotherhood" to members from Rhode Island, New Jersey, and the border states including Illinois and Indiana.[14] As the Conference progressed, Hitchcock noted less rigid attitudes among members of the Ohio delegation,[15] and one radical Congressman complained of Republicans who were "melting away from the neck to the os cocygis."[16]

Delegates generally praised the speechmaking of those who agreed with them. In his reports to Governor Andrew, Goodrich complimented Boutwell's uncompromising reply to Seddon, calling it "the best [speech] that has been made by all odds"; he also liked Baldwin's effort in favor of a national convention and even paid tribute to Reverdy Johnson who gave "a good speech for a southerner."[17] Brockenbrough praised Frelinghuysen's genuinely conciliatory retreat from the Chicago platform;[18] Doniphan lauded the procompromise appeals of Rives, Bronson, and Logan; but, like Brockenbrough, he felt that "by far the most eloquent and able speech" was that of Frelinghuysen. "It was," he said, "chaste, logical, learned, highly ornate & abounded in the most lofty appeals to our patriotism." Doniphan nevertheless noted that he had heard "as able speeches as any of them in Weston, Mo. often."[19]

With a surprising impartiality, Chittenden named Seddon "the most powerful debater of the Conference, skilful, adroit, cunning," with an intense "hatred of all forms of Northern life." His extraordinary appearance suggested the last stages of consumption: "the pallor of his face, his narrow chest, sunken eyes, and attenuated frame." "His voice, husky at first," said Chittenden, "cleared with the excitement of debate, in which he became eloquent."[20]

Speakers relied primarily on either ethical or emotional proof, making little if any effort to support their assertions with statistical evidence. Since almost four-fifths of the members were lawyers, they quite naturally looked for legal precedents and wrangled a great deal over the various interpretations of those who framed the Constitution. Some took delight in displaying their erudition. In a long, tedious exposition, Goodrich insisted that the fathers of the Republic intended to apply the Ordinance of 1787 "to every foot of organized and unorganized territory, wherever situated." At one point Wickliffe exclaimed in exasperation, "No one from Kentucky or Virginia wishes to alter the ordinance of 1787. For God's sake spare us the argument."[21]

Debate focused mainly on slavery and its extension, and on constitutional arrangements designed to maintain political power. No one made a closely reasoned analysis of the economic relationships among the several sections, but some acknowledged the decisive importance of matters such as tariffs and railroads. Clay, for example, found slavery "but an incident to the great questions which are at the bottom of our divisions." "It is, after all," he said, "the old question of the balance of power between the different sections and different interests." Seddon talked bluntly of "the acquisitive disposition" of Northerners, of their greed for land and for office. "The great class of protected interests at the North," he said, "...joined with the landseekers to secure power."[22] At the opposite extreme, James Pollock, an ardent tariff Republican from Pennsylvania, protested that antislavery was not "the leading idea in the platform of his party," and Pleasant A. Hackleman, an Indiana Republican, objected to having "opinions imputed to me and my party which are only entertained by a little knot of fanatical abolitionists."[23]

Slavery, nevertheless, provided delegates with an emotionally charged symbol for rhetorical and political manipulation. The bitter clash between Seddon and Boutwell on February 18 demonstrated the emotional impact of the argument over slavery and its extension. "We hold our *property,* yes, *our property in slaves,* as rightful and as honorable as any property to be found in the broad expanse between ocean and ocean," Seddon insisted. "We feel that in...the protection of the African race, we have a mission to perform, and not a mission only but a right and a duty....In all this time we have contributed far more to the greatness of the North

The Peace Convention, held in Willard's Hotel.
Courtesy of the Library of Congress.

# Scene of the Convention

Exterior of the Convention Hall, Willard's Hotel.
Courtesy of the Library of Congress.

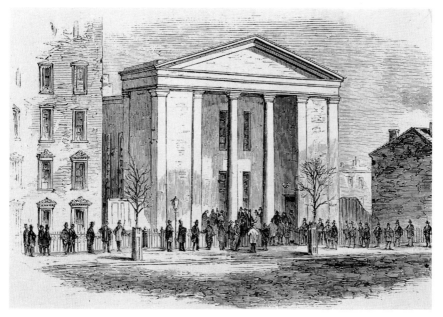

Former President John Tyler,
from Virginia.
President of the Convention.

John C. Wright,
from Ohio.

# Delegates to the Convention

Portrait of John C. Wright, courtesy of the Historical
and Philosophical Society of Ohio; all other portraits,
courtesy of the Library of Congress.

James A. Seddon,
from Virginia.

Thomas Ewing, Sr.,
from Ohio.

George S. Boutwell,
from Massachusetts.

Salmon P. Chase,
from Ohio.

James Guthrie,
from Kentucky.

Charles A. Wickliffe,
from Kentucky.

William C. Rives,
from Virginia.

# TO THE VOTERS OF MICHIGAN!

## READ AND REFLECT.

A vote for the Republican candidates to the Legislature is a vote to return the author of the following infamous letter to the U. S. Senate. Will you return the man, who could deliberately prefer war and "Blood-letting," to a peaceable and honorable arrangement of our difficulties ?

*Washington, February* 11, 1861.

My Dear Governor :—

.Governor Bingham and myself telegraphed you on Saturday, at the request of Massachusetts and New York, to send delegates to the peace or compromise congress. They admit that we were right, and they wrong, *that no Republican State should have sent delegates* ; but they are here and can't get away. Ohio, Indiana, and Rhode Island, are caving in, and there is some doubt of Illinois, and now they beg us, for God's sake, to come to their rescue and

### *save the republican party from rupture.*

I hope you will send stiff-backed men or none. The whole thing was gotten up against my judgement or advice, and will end in thin smoke. Still, I hope, as a matter of courtesy to our erring brethren, that you will send the delegates.

Truly your friend,

**Z. CHANDLER.**

His Excellency, Austin Blair.

P. S.—*Some of the Manufacturing States think that a fight would be awful. Without a little blood-letting this Union would not be worth a rush.*

Zachariah Chandler's "Blood-Letting" Letter. Courtesy of the Manuscript Division of the Library of Congress.

than to our own. Yet all this time we have been assailed, attacked, vilified and defamed, by the people of the North.... Your people thought they were doing GOD a service in signing a petition... for mercy to John Brown and his ruffian invaders of our soil. And when these men met the just reward of their crime... they were looked upon as the victims of oppression, as martyrs to a holy and righteous cause."[24]

Boutwell replied with equal vigor. By his own confession, he "wounded the Southern men sorely" and moved the moderate Mr. Rives to tears. "It is attempted here to put the North on trial," he said of Seddon's speech, "... but I have heard no specification of these charges.... Massachusetts has made war upon slavery wherever she had the right to do it; but much as she *abhors* the institution, she would sacrifice every thing rather than assail it where she has not the right to assail it.... The North will never consent to the separation of the States.... If the Slave States will ... faithfully abide by their constitutional obligations, and remain in the Union until their rights are in *fact* invaded, all will be well. But if they take the responsibility of involving the country in a civil war... but one course remains to those who are true to that Government. They must and will defend it at every sacrifice—if necessary, to the sacrifice of their lives."[25]

If in their rhetoric delegates failed to use all possible means of persuasion, it cannot be attributed to any lack of effort. In the hope that perhaps patriotism might hold the Union together, procompromise orators exploited the American heritage with its common national heroes and its Revolutionary comradeship. "There is scarcely a church spire [in New Jersey]," said Frelinghuysen, "beneath whose shadows does not lay [*sic*] the remains of some of the entombed patriots in that great conflict from both these sections, commingled with those of her own sons!" Both Frelinghuysen and Pollock used the hearthstone theme which Lincoln developed more poetically five days after the Conference adjourned when he appealed to "the mystic chords of memory stretching from every patriot grave to every heart and hearthstone, all over this broad land...." Stockton urged the whole country to rally beneath the glorious folds of stripes and stars.[26]

In appealing to history, Chauncey Cleveland of Connecticut reminded delegates that compromise had once settled the question fairly. Northern radicals testified that they would die for the Union and the Constitution. Moderates both North and South were willing to compromise for the same ends; but each thought of a vastly different document. The Constitution "made for us by WASHINGTON, FRANKLIN, MADISON, and HAMILTON," said Field, speaking grandiloquently for the Northern radicals, "...is good enough for us." Southerners wanted additional assurances. "We are in earnest in our determination to have our rights under the Constitution defined and guaranteed," said J. Dixon Roman of Maryland. "Our safety, as well as our self-respect, requires this."[27]

Since many members had once served together in Congress, there were personal friendships as well as constitutional abstractions to appeal to. Summers pleaded with his former associates for reasonable concessions. "I see a gentleman with whom, for a long time, I was upon terms of peculiar intimacy," he said. "...I appeal to him by every consideration which can move a friend, which can influence a patriot, which can govern the action of a statesman." Ruffin urged members to be brethren, and Stockton called upon Republicans by name, urging them to give up the Chicago platform "to save your country."[28]

Speakers indulged in unabashed flattery. Chase complimented Seddon's ability, sincerity, and frankness; Goodrich praised Southern oratory; Morehead, Northern fairness; Orth lauded Virginia's heritage; Loomis, her justice. Smith appealed to "the venerable and able men around me, who bear historic names." "I have listened to appeals stronger and more eloquent than I ever expect to hear again," Tuck admitted. "The representatives from the South ...are skilful in debate and eloquent in speech." "Were there no [other]...view of the case," he added anticlimactically, "I might become a convert myself."[29]

In Conference deliberations, Southern extremists attempted to avoid the appearance of presenting an ultimatum or threat of secession, but newspaper accounts suggest that Tyler and Seddon urged such a course in Southern caucuses and in private conversations. Seddon, who had advocated the right of secession during the crisis of 1850, was particularly outspoken. Southern moderates made it clear, however, that they vigorously opposed dissolution of the Union. "I *hate* that word secession, because it is a cheat!" said Guthrie. "Call things by their right names! The Southern States

have ... originated a *revolution*." Rives and Reverdy Johnson likewise condemned it, but reminded listeners that "the great fact is
still before us." "Retain the Border States and the seceding States
must come back," Frelinghuysen declared optimistically. "If the
Border States go, I believe war is inevitable."[30]

Realists reminded delegates of the economic interdependence of
the two sections. "We are like two lobes in the same skull," said
Tuck; "one cannot outlive the other." Dodge predicted "certain
and inevitable ruin" unless delegates arrived at an adjustment.
Granger pleaded for some plan that would save the government,
emphasizing the futility of arguing about causes. "Paralysis has
seized the whole country ...," said the former leader of the Silver
Gray Whigs. "The effect is upon us." Guthrie urged Northerners to
consider the Southern economy. "Suppose some event should ...
strike down the value of your property ...," he asked; "would you
not wish to have it restored?" "If disruption—if war must come,
one-half your merchants, one-half your mechanics will become
bankrupt. Not one man, North or South, but must suffer...."[31]

When appeals to patriotism, history, public opinion, friendship,
flattery, and economic advantage failed to produce agreement, extremists and moderates alike impatiently called up the threat of
war. Field, who had already applied to Lincoln for a military commission, foresaw omens of conflict, proclaiming, "Only last night I
dreamed of marching armies and news from the seat of war."
Despite his ominously serious intention, delegates laughed; but he
nevertheless continued, "We must have either the arbitrament of
reason or the arbitrament of the sword."[32] Accurately anticipating
the sentiments of Lincoln's inaugural, Chase asked: "[If] ... the
President does his duty and undertakes to enforce the laws, and
secession or revolution resists, what then? War! Civil war!" Logan
melodramatically described "harvests trampled down," "towns and
villages ... reduced to ... smoking ruins," "widowed wives," and
"orphaned children." "It is a picture that we are doomed to witness," he predicted, "unless we place a restraint upon our passions,
forget selfish interests, and do something to save our country."[33]

Each side took pains to place the onus of war on the other. "If
civil war is brought upon the country," Amaziah B. James of New
York said to Southern extremists, "it will be your work, not ours."
Stockton listed the inducements "with which the Republican lead-

ers would seduce the North into fratricidal war":

The expenditure of uncounted millions, the distribution of epaulets and military commissions for an army of half a million of men, the immense patronage involved in the letting of army contracts, the inflation of prices and the rise of property which would follow the excessive issue of paper money, made necessary by the lavish expenditure;— these, indeed, are the enormous bribes which the Republican party offers.[34]

Southerners, even Southern moderates, looked upon federal coercion as war. Comparing it to the John Brown raid, J. M. Morehead warned: "If the new President proposes to come down to the South and conquer us, he will find that the whole temple shall fall." Seddon likewise insisted that "Virginia *will not permit coercion*"—a position which Lot Morrill interpreted as "an attitude of menace." "It gives aid and comfort," he said, "to those who trample upon the laws and defy the authority of this Government."[35]

At this point, Stockton shouted "Silence, sir!" and "rushed toward Senator Morrill with violent and angry gesticulations." "We will not permit our Southern friends to be charged with bad faith . . .! No black Republican shall——" Twenty or thirty Republican stalwarts then reportedly surrounded Morrill "like a living wall." Southerners similarly rallied around Stockton, and a disgraceful brawl was prevented only by the prompt intervention of President Tyler. "Order," he shouted. "Shame upon the delegate who would dishonor this Conference with violence."[36]

Since their soil was the obvious battleground, representatives of the border states had greatest reason to speak the language of compromise. Ruffin called attention to fourteen hundred miles of "what is virtually a frontier" along the southern Tennessee and North Carolina borders. Rives told of the unhappy geographical circumstance which placed them "between two embattled regions, between two angry, excited, and hostile portions of the Union." "We wish to stay the hands of the extremists on both sides," said John W. Crisfield of Maryland. "We wish to stand by the Union." Though a Republican, Frelinghuysen was willing to " 'back down' to save the country." "Two gentlemen cannot live in a parlor together a single day without reciprocal compromises," he observed metaphorically. "Our Government itself was a compromise. . . ." Ewing advised delegates to be "firm as a rock in battle, but conciliatory in council." "When the country is in danger," boasted Rodman M. Price of New Jersey, "my political robes hang loosely on my shoulders."[37]

When it became apparent that extremists would not, as they put it, sacrifice their principles, the compromisers talked despairingly of the failure of speechmaking. "All the speeches that have been made, and all the declamation that has been uttered on this floor," Thomas White of Pennsylvania concluded, "have not made a single convert." After fifteen days of deliberation, Franklin T. Backus of Ohio observed that "discussion, so far, has tended very little toward harmony or unanimity." Cleveland called for a stop to "long speeches and picking flaws in each other." "If we stay here and make speeches until doomsday, we shall be no better off," he asserted. "I am for action, and coming to an immediate decision." Price concurred. "Do not let us sit here," he said, "like the great Belshazzar till the handwriting appears on the wall." "Give us your votes," pleaded Wickliffe as the Conference drew to a close. "We have had enough of discussion, which amounts to nothing."[38]

## Chapter Eight

# Stiff-Backed Men—or None

Fearful that perhaps a majority might heed such appeals and endorse the Guthrie report, radicals sent out a desperate call for more help. Goodrich bluntly stated the anticompromise predicament in one of his faithful dispatches to Governor Andrew: "We don[']t want these Union savers and Democrats, united with the South, to vote us Republicans down."[1] To avoid this possibility, Chase, Wadsworth, and Field organized an appeal for recruits from Michigan, Minnesota, Wisconsin, and Kansas.[2] Senators Zachariah Chandler and Kingsley S. Bingham of Michigan responded by urging Governor Austin Blair to get true, unflinching delegates from the Wolverine State at once. Chandler telegraphed the Governor, and then explained the urgency of the situation in a subsequent letter:

> Ohio, Indiana, and Rhode Island, are caving in, and there is some doubt of Illinois, and now they [Massachusetts and New York] beg us, for God's sake, to come to their rescue and SAVE THE REPUBLICAN PARTY FROM RUPTURE.
>
> I hope you will send stiff-backed men or none.

In a postscript, Chandler noted that "some of the Manufacturing States think that a fight would be awful." "Without a little blood-letting," the Senator concluded, "this nation would not be worth a rush."[3]

In a message which aroused much confusion and excitement, Governor Blair promptly urged the Michigan Legislature to reconsider its previous action, indicating changed circumstances affecting the propriety of sending commissioners.[4] The Ann Arbor *Michigan Argus,* which earlier had denounced the Republican-controlled Legislature for its rampant fanaticism and mulish obstinacy in failing to send commissioners, now called Blair's request for ultra-abolitionized commissioners a new disunionist act in the farce which had been on stage for almost two weeks in Lansing. Blair's man Friday in the Legislature, Charles V. DeLand of Jackson, attempted to read a fellow Republican out of the party for having dared to favor the appointment of commissioners.[5] A Democratic member of the House boldly threatened to resist Republican coercion: "... if abolitionism ... should attempt an anti-slavery war against the South," he asserted, "it would be assailed with a fire in the rear." Radicals branded such sentiments as traitorous, but replied in language just as combustible. "We have fed the [Southern] whiners with sugar plums long enough," said the Marshall *Statesman;* "if they have the *pysora* now, we would recommend ... a mixture of sulphur and nitre—an infallible remedy in desperate cases."[6]

In attempting to gain support for a delegation, Blair indiscreetly showed Chandler's letter to several of his partisans in the Legislature, and somehow it fell into the unfriendly hands of a Democratic member who read it on the floor of the House. "Whether they got into my office & found it or some fool of a member let him read it I cannot tell nor is it material," Blair said in an explanation to Chandler. "There is not a sentiment in it which is not creditable to you.... I write this that you may know precisely what is the truth —it plagues me though I hope it will not you."[7]

Democrats, of course, persistently plagued Chandler and his party, attacking its program of "blood, carnage, eternal dissolution and universal ruin." The *Detroit Free Press* headlined the story of his bloodletting letter, as: TREASON—A PLOT TO BETRAY THE COUNTRY—BLAIR, CHANDLER AND BINGHAM IN CONSPIRACY— THE COMMISSIONER QUESTION REVIVED WITH TREASONABLE INTENT.[8] "Is not Michigan proud of such a Senator?" asked the Hillsdale *County Democrat.* "... An *Ass*-tute statesman."[9]

Looking upon a compromise with the slave oligarchy as a

calamity more to be dreaded than civil war itself, Wolverine radicals remained suspicious of the Conference even though their leaders urged representation.[10] When a purported version of Senator Bingham's letter was read in the House, it brought more Democratic hostility than Republican support: "If Michigan were now represented on the floor of the [Peace] convention," the Senator argued, "she would hold the balance of power and could prevent compromise."[11] With the Democrats now in opposition, the House defeated a resolution to have the Governor appoint delegates 40 to 37; and an amendment to appoint Chandler and Bingham failed 40 to 34.[12] Blair thought it "shabby...not to have acceded to the request of our true friends." "The truth is," he wrote Chandler, "the members are so afraid of the shadow of backing down that they do not dare do anything. I said to one of them, 'Are you afraid of Chandler?' said he 'I am afraid of every body. I would not trust *myself* in that damned Conference.' "[13]

Claiming that the radicals in the Legislature misrepresented their constituents, Democrats urged the appointment of delegates by popular action. Late in January in Detroit, where financial interests favored a speedy resolution of the secession crisis, a grand Union demonstration with an immense audience passed resolutions endorsing Crittenden's Compromise, thus giving substance to the contention that the people were ready for a peaceful adjustment.[14] In February, prominent men of all parties supported another such meeting for the purpose of dispatching a delegation. The *Free Press* urged the Republican mayor of Detroit to take the initiative in this matter without delay and thus make himself exceedingly popular. The mayor failed to act, however; and when the Democratic state convention met in Detroit in mid-February, members decided to send procompromise resolutions rather than delegates to Willard's Hall.[15]

In Minnesota, radicals were ready to fight rather than to surrender their rights, thoughts, and opinions in a union with "Southern robbers and traitors." Like Senator Chandler, the editor of the Saint Paul *Minnesotian* announced, "Before this rampant fever of disunion will at all abate, THERE MUST BE BLOOD-LETTING!"[16] Politicians of the North Star State talked idealistically of principles, but they also demonstrated an understandable desire for patronage. "When once our fingers clutch the turkey we have fairly bagged, must we not only relinquish our hold," asked the editor of the Saint Peter *Tribune* in familiar frontier imagery, "but be compelled to pay the slave-holders something handsome for snatching it from us?" A few conservatives favored an amicable arrangement with the South, but the Chatfield *Republican* dismissed them as "Loafers, Black-guards, Nuisances, Cowards, and the Corruption of our midst generally."[17]

In the November elections, Republicans had carried the state by an almost 2-to-1 margin, with Lincoln winning in all but five of the forty-six counties. Republicans controlled the state Senate, 19 to 2; the House, 40 to 2. Virginia's appeal for a Conference thus fell on unsympathetic ears. The Saint Paul *Press* charged that she made her proposal with love on her lips and hatred in her heart, and legislators showed no inclination whatsoever to accept.[18] One waggish Senator suggested the Chicago platform as the basis of adjustment; another introduced an amendment requiring delegates to pay their own way. House members considered the possibility of appointing three discreet and reputable citizens, who would guarantee their adherence to the Chicago platform by posting a ten-thousand-dollar bond.[19]

When Governor Alexander H. Ramsey transmitted Senator Morton S. Wilkinson's request from Washington for radical recruits, legislators considered the invitation more seriously. After defeating numerous alternative proposals, the Senate voted 13 to 6 for a resolution allowing the Governor to appoint delegates with the consent of the Senate. Members rejected the basis of adjustment suggested by Virginia as not acceptable to the free states, and instructed delegates to oppose the extension of slavery into the territories. By a vote of 30 to 8, however, the House refused to recognize in any manner the existence of a so-called Peace Convention. The Senate concurred in the House substitute, but added an amendment suggesting a national convention, which the House refused to accept by a vote of 29 to 6. "It is not expedient to compromise," the resolution said, "when the only basis is for the protection of slavery."[20]

Sentiment was no less militant in Wisconsin than in Minnesota or Michigan. In January, Governor Alexander Randall had "stirred up the people 'from the bottom' " with a bellicose inaugural, declaring, "... secession is revolution: revolution is war: War against the government...is treason." Editors reiterated the no compromise slogans of Horace Greeley and were rewarded with the honor of having their editorials republished in the *Tribune*. "Let our Commissioners go to Washington and humiliate themselves before the minions of Slavery," warned the editor of the Whitewater *Register* in a careless metaphor, "...but when they return...they will hear the mutterings of that storm that shall bury them forever in political oblivion...." Republicans held majorities of more than 2 to 1 in both houses, sufficient certainly to prevent the dispatch of delegates, providing there were no weak-kneed members.[21]

Because of the financial crisis, urban Republicans representing commercial interests generally took a more conciliatory position than their rural colleagues. The Democratic United States Attorney in Wisconsin assured Governor Letcher of Virginia that moderate Republicans of the Milwaukee Board of Trade hoped to induce the Legislature to answer Virginia's invitation by sending "practicable men as Commissioners." "The Republican party [here]... has been controuled [*sic*] by more ultra abolitionists, than any other state except perhaps Michigan," he explained; "yet a large portion of this party are believed to be reasonable in their individual views...and appear now to be determined to make an effort." Hoping to gain converts among this group, Democrats talked of organinzing *"a great Union-saving compromise party."*[22]

Governor Randall submitted Virginia's invitation to the Legislature on January 29, and two weeks of controversy followed. In the Assembly, members argued about the expediency of sending a delegation, its proper instruction, its method of selection, its personnel, and its pay—if any. There were filibusters and calls of the House. The *Argus and Democrat* noted about as bad a tangle as a legislative body ever got into. Although its majority report opposed acceptance as a compromise of the honor and dignity of the state, the Assembly nevertheless passed a resolution authorizing the Governor to appoint commissioners who were to take as a basis of settlement the distinctly expressed will of the people. In spite of a "bull of ex-communication" against all who favored the resolution, twenty-five erratic Republicans joined with the Democrats to provide a majority of 49 to 41.[23]

The Senate majority report recommended indefinite postponement, asserting it would be worse than idle pastime to depute commissioners to attend such a conference. Republican Buel E. Hutchinson, however, argued that Wisconsin delegates might help to secure honorable terms of peace or prevent dishonorable terms of capitulation. Six Republicans endorsed this view and voted with eight Democrats for a resolution authorizing a delegation appointed by the Legislature. A 14-to-14 tie resulted, which Republican Lieutenant Governor Butler G. Noble broke by voting to accept Virginia's invitation. "We must save the Border States," Noble wrote Weed, adding, "...I am 'catching fits' from the abolition 'wing'...."[24]

Although both houses had passed separate resolutions favoring representation, they found it difficult to agree upon whether the Governor or the Legislature should appoint commissioners, as well as other details. On February 13, the Assembly laid the whole matter on the table, defeating it at least for the time being, just as radicals in Washington were making their appeal for reinforcements.[25] What was described as a sensation involving Carl Schurz no doubt contributed to the parliamentary impasse.

When news of a Peace Conference was first announced, Schurz found himself in Norwalk, Ohio, on a lecture tour. He immediately telegraphed Governor Randall: "Appoint commissioners—me one—to help our side." Randall found cause to make public this cryptic document, and Schurz's law partner hastened to disclaim it as a base forgery. Democrats solicited the testimony of the Norwalk operator, who replied, "I know Mr. Carl Schurz. He handed me the dispatch himself." The telegrapher's response and the resulting furor prompted Schurz to justify what Democrats were ridiculing as his ludicrous exhibition of vanity. "Certainly, I *did* send that dispatch, and I must confess I am at a loss to understand the anxiety my friends seem to feel about it," he announced in a letter written for publication. "...I suggested my own appointment because I flattered myself that I might be able...to give to the feelings of a large majority of the people of Wisconsin, a tolerably fair and forcible expression....What may have induced the Governor to spread a private dispatch before the public in so conspicuous a manner, I have no means of judging....But I am far from interpreting this act of Gov. Randall as an attempt to 'make capital against me'; for I ask you in candor, what capital can there be made of it?"[26]

The editor of the *Wisconsin State Journal* thought the reply acquitted Schurz of the charge of presumptuous self-importance; but Democrats continued to snicker, reminding Republicans that his own partner was ashamed of the telegram. The *Patriot,* for example, wondered, "Does Carl's admission make it all right 'for our side'?"[27]

Apparently undaunted, Schurz sent another telegraphic dispatch calling for a Republican caucus on February 19. Arriving in Madison on the evening train just before the meeting convened, Schurz hurried to the scene in time to deliver a speech urging that the Republican members of Congress be authorized to sit in the Peace Conference. Since he had recently visited the President-elect in Springfield, he knowingly assured his listeners that Mr. Lincoln and our truest Republicans in Washington desired increased radical representation. After a spirited discussion, the Republican members rejected Schurz's appeal, partly no doubt because "his action savored strongly of presumption and dictation." The waggish editor of the *Argus and Democrat* headlined the results of this bootless errand: NO COMMISSIONERS TO WASHINGTON—"OUR SIDE" NOT STRENGTHENED.[28]

On February 20, after elected officials had failed to act, Union men and Democratic members of the Legislature organized a statewide meeting at the Assembly hall in Madison for the purpose of electing commissioners. They urged all friendly to the project, regardless of party to participate, claiming that nobody in office could speak for the people of the state. The *Argus and Democrat* admitted that the meeting would have little practical effect, but predicted that it would lead to a breakup of all existing political organizations. The meeting was held on February 26, as scheduled, and three Republicans and two Democrats were selected as peace commissioners: Marshall M. Strong, Mason C. Dodge, John H. Tweedy, Hercules L. Dousman, and Nelson Dewey. The *Wisconsin State Journal* described the participants as " 'the very blossom and fragrancy' of that peculiar class of men who manipulate Democratic conventions"; when the Peace Conference adjourned next day, the *Journal* taunted: "Will the commissioners appointed by the Democratic-Seward-Union Meeting . . . persist in starting for Washington . . . next week?"[29]

Kansas, admitted at last to statehood on January 29, 1861, after over five years of conflict, was also solicited for stiff-backed support. Senator Trumbull in fact testified that its admission had been rushed through for the very purpose of getting radical help in Congress, where two additional votes might determine the fate of the country.[30] From January 29 to February 9, territorial officials acted as interim officers of the state. Since the state Legislature was not in session, the acting governor dispatched James C. Stone, president of the Leavenworth, Pawnee, and Western Railroad, and Thomas Ewing, Jr., newly elected Chief Justice of the Kansas Supreme Court, as commissioners. He signed the appointing document "George M. Beebe, Gov." and assigned the ambiguous date, "February."[31]

Arriving at Willard's on February 22 ahead of Ewing, Stone presented the document signed by Beebe and thereby initiated a debate over credentials. Suspecting that they had caught a tartar rather than a sympathetic ally, radicals opposed his admission. Rising to a question of privilege, Field objected to seating Stone because, as he said, "It looks as though the gentleman was sent here only for the purpose of giving the vote to certain propositions." Since Field had joined in sending the telegrams requesting anticompromise delegates, he was qualified to register such a complaint. Stone modestly observed that he had no desire to force himself into the Conference and withdrew. Field then forced through a resolution requesting the credentials committee to report the facts concerning Stone's appointment.[32]

Sometime after the inauguration of state officials in Kansas on February 9, the new governor, Charles Robinson, appointed two additional delegates, Henry J. Adams, a rival Republican candidate for the gubernatorial nomination, and Martin Conway, once an attorney for John Brown and now the Congressman from Kansas. When the three remaining commissioners arrived at Willard's on February 23, the credentials committee resolved the dispute by accepting both delegations.[33]

Once in Washington, the four delegates from the Jayhawk State took far more interest in Kansas land and railroad speculation than they did in abstract constitutional questions. Though appointed by acting Governor Beebe, Tom Ewing, Jr., was in Washington primarily to help Governor Robinson become Commissioner of Indian Affairs—an appointment which would enable them to control the railroad interests of the state.[34] Conway represented an opposing faction headed by James H. Lane, a candidate for the United States Senate; his assignment was to make an arrangement with Lincoln whereby all appointments in Kansas might be withheld until after the state Legislature convened and elected Senators who, it was hoped, might keep the federal patronage out of Governor Robinson's hands.[35]

The radical appeal for recruits thus brought only one unreliable delegation—and angry feuding which threatened to disrupt their party. "It is," said the *New York Times,* "one of the most discouraging features of our time, that, just as the Republican Party is about to assume the power for which it has been striving . . . its members should fall to warring upon each other, with far more ferocity than they ever brought to the crusade against the common enemy."[36]

## Chapter Nine

# An Uncertain Victory

While Republicans in Wisconsin, Minnesota, and Michigan argued over whether or not to reinforce their partisans at Willard's, the Conference devoted itself to speechmaking. From February 15 to 22, delegates did little to bring about action on the Guthrie Committee report. In the hope that patriotism might overwhelm partisanship on Washington's Birthday, Wickliffe moved to end debate and proceed to a vote. Although his hope proved to be unduly optimistic, delegates did on that auspicious day begin a more or less systematic consideration of the proposals before them, taking up each of the seven sections of the majority report in turn.[1]

Radicals continued to delay action by introducing amendments seemingly designed more to annoy Southern members than to solve delicate constitutional problems. Wilmot wanted the United States to make full compensation to citizens who suffered from the action of mobs and riotous assemblies in the slave states; Asa Fowler of New Hampshire saw no reason for requiring the consent of Maryland to the abolition of slavery in the District, and so moved to delete this stipulation from the report. Charles J. McCurdy of Connecticut offered an amendment to prevent the sale of slaves in the waters of New York, thus proposing to prohibit in the Constitution, as Samuel Ames of Rhode Island said, a right which no one wishes to exercise. In one of his rare appearances at the Conference, Daniel E. Somes of Maine introduced an amendment guaranteeing freedom of speech in the territories. Phrased in highly unparliamentary language, the amendment provided that "people ... be left perfectly free to discuss the subject of slavery." On behalf of the Northwest, William Vandever of Iowa moved to guarantee freedom of navigation on the Mississippi.[2]

Extreme Southern rights advocates likewise offered amendments which aroused hostility and which were perhaps calculated for later use in justifying secession. David S. Reid of North Carolina wanted a constitutional recognition of property in slaves. Seddon similarly wanted "the words 'master and slave' somewhere inserted ... in plain English language, ... so that the Constitution shall, beyond any question, recognize the relation."[3] Aylett H. Buckner of Missouri proposed an amendment prohibiting the federal government from coercing or making war directly or indirectly upon a state.[4] Less objectionable to Yankees, but nevertheless time-consuming, was James B. Clay's motion to substitute the Crittenden resolutions "without the crossing of a 't' or the dotting of an 'i.' " Delegates who took the trouble to inspect Clay's resolution discovered several additional provisions quite foreign to those introduced by the Kentucky Senator.[5]

Northern and Southern moderates generally opposed tampering with the majority report on the grounds that it would destroy all hope of an ultimate agreement. "I hope we shall reject all such amendments," said Guthrie of one hair-splitting motion. "I consider this simply procrastination." Rives dismissed them as "abstract questions thrust upon us." "They would," he said, "better befit a debating society than an assembly of statesmen met to consider constitutional questions."[6]

As Lincoln made his circuitous way to Washington, Southern delegates suspected that Republican obstructionism was related somehow to his arrival. "The Convention cannot move a wheel until Lincoln gets here," Doniphan wrote. "If he is under Seward's guidance we will compromise in a day—if he is under the Chase and Greely [sic] faction, then we may go home and tell Gabriel to blow for the nation will be dissolved in a few days or months at most...."[7] Lincoln's speeches en route, particularly his Indianapolis speech, gave encouragement to the radicals and led moderates to feel that nothing would be conceded.[8] In a conversation with the President-elect in Albany, Weed was discouraged by his inflexibility. The Albany editor, who had been seeking an adjustment in behalf of New York financial interests, communicated the results of his interview to Seward:

> I had an hour with Mr. L. yesterday. The conversation was confined to a single point, in relation to which I have no reason to suppose that he listened with profit. . . . I should like to tell you what was said, and what views are entertained, but of course cannot on paper. My solicitude in reference to the Country is not diminished. . . . He has not, as I supposed, consulted with Judge Logan [head of the Illinois delegation]. You have a delicate duty before you.[9]

Since Weed prided himself on saying much in a few words in corresponding with Seward, he did not make explicit the nature of this delicate duty, but it may have involved negotiating a satisfactory Peace Conference adjustment with Lincoln, Logan, and members of the Illinois delegation as principals.

In any event, Seward played an important role in hurrying Lincoln through Baltimore by what the Albany *Atlas and Argus* described as the Underground Railroad and headlined as, MORE ASS-ASS-IN-NATION.[10] Among the many rumors explaining Lincoln's surreptitious flight to Washington was the account of the New York *Express* relating it to the Peace Conference:

> The early arrival here on Saturday of Mr. Lincoln was brought about by the condition of things in the Peace Convention. Dispatches were received from Richmond, Va., announcing that the Union men would have to submit to Secession unless information was sent them immediately of what would be the probable result of the final vote on the report of the Committee. The Virginians were informed that the report would be passed, but without the great State of New York. As this was deemed unsatisfactory by the Union men of Virginia, Lincoln was telegraphed to come to Washington immediately. This he did, and he was met at the [Willard's] hotel at 6 A.M. by Senator Seward, who briefly related to him the state of affairs. Mr. Lincoln, up to the present, has not consented to authorize Senator Seward to speak . . . in favor of the report, but it is thought . . . that he will do so to-day or tomorrow.[11]

Greeley's *Tribune* disavowed the story, denying that any such miraculous transformation could possibly take place in Lincoln's attitude on the extension of slavery. "Away with such compromises!" cried Greeley, annoyed no doubt to hear that Seward had Lincoln's attention.[12]

To accommodate the President-elect, the Willard brothers hastily evacuated William E. Dodge from their most desirable suite of rooms adjoining Parlor Six. Although fatigued with travel and very hoarse, Lincoln went with Seward to call on President Buchanan and then began an exhausting series of interviews. Chittenden obtained an appointment to brief him on the personnel and the activities of the Peace Conference, and the President-elect indicated a particular desire to meet Mr. Rives, Judge Ruffin, and members with whom he had served in Congress. Using Seward as intermediary, Hiland Hall of the uncompromising Vermont delegation submitted a surprising, but earnest, confidential letter suggesting that it "would be a noble act of conciliation & nothing more" to submit the Guthrie report to the people. Offsetting this advice was that of Francis P. Blair, Sr., who, according to report, called to counsel "anything but peaceful measures."[13]

Under the same roof at the Peace Conference, Judge Logan moved that President Tyler call upon the President-elect and request an interview for the entire body. Although Chittenden recalled cries of "No! No! Vote it down," the motion was passed unanimously. Ignoring his instructions, Tyler sent a note rather than calling in person, but Lincoln promptly replied that he would be pleased to receive the members at nine that evening or at any other time which suited their convenience. Accordingly, the interview was arranged at nine, allowing Lincoln time for dinner with incoming Vice-President Hamlin at Senator Seward's residence.[14]

At the appointed time, only fifteen hours after his unceremonious arrival, Lincoln received the assembled members in Parlor Six. Chase introduced Tyler first, then the others. Lincoln provided a pleasantry of some sort with each handshake: "Your name is all the endorsement you require," he told James B. Clay, son of his former idol. "You cannot be a disunionist," he said to Summers, "unless your nature has changed since we met in Congress." "You are a smaller man than I supposed," was his tactless witticism to Rives; "I mean in person: everyone is acquainted with the greatness of your intellect."[15]

After the introductions, delegates remained for an animated exchange of ideas. Lincoln spoke "apparently without premeditation" and "with a singular ease and facility of expression." Rives insisted, "Everything now depends upon you." Lincoln disagreed, suggesting that *all* might try "obedience to the Constitution." Seddon complained about the abolitionists, "your John Browns and your Garrisons," and the incendiary Northern press; Lincoln observed that John Brown had died on the gallows and wondered if Northerners were peculiar in supporting a free press. Understandably worried about business conditions, Dodge said, "It is for you, sir, to say whether the grass shall grow in the streets of our commercial cities." "If it depends upon me," Lincoln replied, "the grass will not grow anywhere except in the fields and the meadows." When Dodge interpreted this to mean, "You will not go to war on account of slavery," Lincoln sternly added that, in accordance with his oath, the Constitution must be "respected, obeyed, enforced, and defended, let the grass grow where it may."[16]

Republicans, particularly the radicals, greeted these remarks with surprised satisfaction. Since Lincoln had been widely heralded as "a *simple Susan*"[17] without "manners" or "social grace,"[18] "an ignorant country buffoon,"[19] if not in fact "an ass in a lion's skin,"[20] his partisans took comfort in this tangible evidence of his capacity. Although dismayed by his uncompromising position, which Ruffin called a misfortune, Southern moderates were somewhat encouraged to find him less threatening than he had been described in the papers. Rives, for example, concluded that he had "been both misjudged and misunderstood by the Southern people."[21]

When delegates reconvened on Monday, February 25, the radicals displayed no less militancy. If Lincoln gave any word, it was apparently the watchword, "Stand firm." McCurdy's "useless" proposition passed 11 to 10; and Guthrie exclaimed bitterly, "We shall get nothing here that is satisfactory to the people of the south side of the river." Turner pacified him temporarily by moving a reconsideration, but soon later the dejected Kentuckian announced: "I feel that my mission here is ended and that I may as well withdraw from the Conference.... The report of the committee is not satisfactory to the South; it is even doubtful whether they will adopt it; certainly they will not, if it is cut to pieces by amendments." The *Report* made no mention of it, but newspapers claimed that he became so offended that he left the hall, signifying an intention not to return. Influenced perhaps by his dramatic, but momentary absence, delegates defeated the McCurdy amendment 14 to 7 on reconsideration.[22]

Despite the many proposals, few basic changes went into the majority report. New Jersey and Rhode Island, sometimes Ohio and Pennsylvania, and occasionally even Illinois and Indiana voted with the South to lay on the table or defeat most amendments, thus leaving, as the *Detroit Free Press* said, "substantially Mr. Guthrie's proposition with modified verbiage."[23] SECTION 1 restoring the Missouri Compromise line was rephrased by Thomas E. Franklin of Pennsylvania and amended to apply specifically to present territory only. SECTION 2 on the acquisition of territory was amended so as to reduce the required Senate majority from four-fifths to two-thirds, providing this total included a majority of Senators from the free states and a majority from the slaveholding states. SECTION 3 guaranteeing involuntary servitude where it existed was rephrased, and the prohibition of rights of transit and sale made explicit. SECTION 4 remained unchanged. SECTION 5 was rephrased and the importation of coolies, as well as slaves, prohibited. SECTION 6 was amended so that SECTION 2, as well as one, three, and five, might not be amended without the unanimous consent of all the states. SECTION 7 concerning fugitive slaves was rephrased so that payment for fugitives rescued by mobs "shall preclude further claim to such fugitive"; and a provision was added to implement Article IV, Section 2 of the Constitution: "Congress shall provide by law for securing to the citizens of each State the privileges and immunities of citizens in the several States."*

Both minority reports failed. Indiana, New Jersey, Ohio, Pennsylvania, Rhode Island, and Kansas voted with the South to defeat Baldwin's proposal for a national convention 13 to 8. Despite an earnest appeal by Chase, delegates defeated by a vote of 11 to 9 Tuck's substitute, also calling for a convention. Even the Ohio delegation voted with the opposition. Tyler left the chair and was courteously granted an extension of time to support Seddon's proposals in an elaborate speech, but the motion nevertheless lost

---

* Complete text of the proposed Constitutional Amendment XIII may be found in the Appendix.

16 to 4, with only Virginia, North Carolina, Tennessee, and Missouri favoring it.[24]

On February 26, the eighteenth day of sitting, after a session lasting until 2:00 A.M. the night before, time came for a vote on the majority report as amended. The crucial decision, of course, came on SECTION 1. In an appeal to the radicals early in the Conference, Reverdy Johnson had summarized the issue: "I tell you it is we who are yielding. By the decision of the Supreme Court we have the right to go North of this line with our slaves. Now, all we ask you to give us here is the territory south of that line; and even as to that, we give you the right to destroy slavery there whenever a State organized out of it chooses to do so. We are, in fact, yielding to you. We abandon our rights North. Will you not let us retain what is already ours, South?"[25] Southern extremists objected because it did not apply to territory hereafter acquired, as did the Crittenden propositions, and for the very reasons Johnson indicated: they wanted all the territories open to slavery, just as the radicals wanted them all free.

The vote took place "in the midst of much partially suppressed excitement," with "sharp remarks of dissent or approval" after the poll of each state. Brockenbrough joined Seddon and Tyler to outvote Rives and Summers, thus casting Virginia against it. Reid, Barringer, and George S. Davis outvoted moderates Ruffin and Morehead in the North Carolina delegation. Doniphan, Buckner, and Waldo P. Johnson outvoted Harrison Hough and John D. Coalter in the Missouri delegation. Thus strong Southern rights advocates joined with radicals Chase, Field, Goodrich, Boutwell, and the rest to defeat the essential provision of the majority report 11 to 8.[26]

A disagreeable silence followed the announcement of the result. Then came several minutes of confusion during which Boutwell recalled that some of the border-state men wept like children. "The result they must have anticipated," he explained, "but they had been wrought to a high condition of nervous excitement...." Turner, the pivotal member of the divided Illinois delegation, moved a reconsideration. Granger rebuked "those gentlemen from the slave states especially," charging them with "the awful responsibility" of plunging the nation into war. Then he moved an adjournment to give recalcitrants a little time for consideration.[27]

When the Conference reconvened that evening, Wickliffe immediately moved another adjournment. "I hope after some of the informal consultations which have been held since the adjournment...this afternoon," he explained, "that we may yet be able to bring our minds together, and to adopt the propositions recommended by the committee."[28]

While delegates caucused in private rooms or milled about the crowded lobbies, partisans of the various factions intensified their pressures on the recently arrived Westerner in Parlor Six. Joshua R. Giddings, the militant Ohio abolitionist, arrived to make, as he said, "my influence felt on the great subject that has occupied my life." Greeley came down from New York and received a three-hour interview, to the exclusion of all others.[29] A group headed by Senator Preston King received an audience to urge "*strongly* the necessity of an *uncompromising* policy," and left with assurances that were "entirely satisfactory."[30] Since these radicals wanted jobs as well as adherence to the Chicago platform, the ideological controversy became inextricably involved in the serious business of Cabinet making.

Conservatives exerted a corresponding pressure. Governor Hicks of Maryland reportedly threatened secession if the Conference adjourned without doing anything. After noting that they both had sons, Senator Douglas begged Lincoln to intervene with his friends in the Conference. An unconfirmed newspaper report indicated that Lincoln held a meeting to consider the appeal.[31] In another interview of several hours' duration, Guthrie, Doniphan, Summers, Rives, and C. S. Morehead attempted to persuade him to interpose for a settlement. Emphasizing "the dreadful impending danger," Morehead "*implored*" him to avert it." Later, Morehead recalled that Rives' appeal was characterized by a dignity and an eloquence seldom surpassed.[32]

Moderate editors noted that Lincoln became more liberal in an environment removed from the Illinois land speculators, but they presented no evidence to demonstrate that he had retreated from his inflexible position on the territorial question—the substance of SECTION 1.[33] Palmer said that Lincoln "advised us to deal as liberally as possible," but warned against "any concession in the face of a menace." Weed told Governor Morgan that the President-elect was less inclined to pursue a conciliatory course than he had hoped. "I am not at all satisfied," Weed said, "with the *general* aspect of things here."[34]

When delegates assembled next morning, February 27, radicals in the New York delegation found themselves without their previous majority because of the absence of David Dudley Field, who had been called to argue a case before the Supreme Court. At a caucus before he left, the delegation decided by a vote of 6 to 5 that New York should cast its ballot "solid against each of the pending propositions." When John A. King, the temporary chairman, proposed to announce the vote as decided, minority members threatened a protest, noting that with Field absent the delegation was divided equally.[35] King explained the awkward circumstances on the Conference floor and requested permission to cast the vote as determined in caucus; Corning objected; and Tyler ruled that "an absent member cannot participate in the control of a vote except by general leave of the Convention." No one appealed his decision, and the vote of New York thus was not recorded.[36]

The Kansas delegation was also divided and consequently abstained from both the first vote and the reconsideration of SECTION 1. Although Indiana voted on all the other sections of the report, her delegates avoided a commitment on this section, using the instructions from their Legislature as an excuse. Missouri, which had opposed the proposition 3 to 2 the previous afternoon, now declined to vote. "The whole thing being a sort of shapeless mass," Doniphan explained, none of the Missouri members had in fact favored it; but, on reconsideration, they unanimously decided that the proposals "should go before the country for what they were worth" without Missouri's sanction.[37]

Despite warnings from the *Illinois State Journal* against a base surrender of principle, Illinois changed its vote from No to Yes, leaving a majority of 9 to 8 in favor of the essential provision of the Guthrie report.[38] Rumors heralded Lincoln's intervention in behalf of a negotiated adjustment, and his private secretary talked mysteriously of some occult influence which had contributed to the dramatic reversal.[39] The delegates, however, insisted that they alone were responsible. "Judge Palmer and myself of our own volition," said Turner in a letter of explanation to Lincoln, "... agreed to co-opperate [*sic*] with Judge Logan in moving a reconsideration." Palmer later indicated some uneasiness about his vote.

"I told Mr. Lincoln, before I left Washington," he jokingly recalled, "that I would have to go into the army, in order to prove ... that I was a sincere anti-slavery man."[40]

After this uncertain victory, procompromise supporters found less difficulty with the remaining provisions, all of which passed without the excitement occasioned by SECTION 1. Four Northern states—New Jersey, Rhode Island, Ohio, and Pennsylvania—and four border states—Maryland, Tennessee, Kentucky, and Delaware—voted for every provision. Thanks to Logan, Palmer, and Turner, Illinois supported six of the seven provisions. Despite their pledges to Governor Morton and their instructions to report to the Legislature before voting, a majority of the Indiana delegation supported four of the seven. New York was deadlocked on every vote but one; Kansas on all but two. Maine and Iowa opposed every provision; Massachusetts, six of the seven; New Hampshire, Vermont, Connecticut, and North Carolina, five; and Virginia, four.*

Moderates Rives and Summers of Virginia and John M. Morehead and Ruffin of North Carolina dissented from the votes of their respective states; and Clay of Kentucky and A. W. O. Totten of Tennessee dissented from the procompromise positions of their delegations. Radicals Chase and Wolcott of Ohio, Wilmot and Meredith of Pennsylvania, Hackleman and Orth of Indiana, and Cook of Illinois likewise registered dissents.[41]

Vindictive partisans looked about for someone to blame. "The great mistake," Goodrich wailed, "is in Gov. Curtin and Gov. Dennison sending so many conservatives." Wolcott sent Dennison an angry telegram: "I consider the plan as a surrender to the Slave Holders of vital principles[.] All of the Ohio Commissioners except Chase & myself voted for every feature of the Compromise." The *New York Tribune* attributed the failure to an unexpected accident, Field's absence.[42] The like-minded *Chicago Tribune* blamed the northwestern state legislatures: "If Minnesota, Wisconsin and Michigan had sent commissioners, ... *as all the Republicans in Congress earnestly desired them to do,* the pot of devils' broth ... cooked in Willard's ball-room would have been spoiled, and several men who have there grown weak in the knees and caved in, would have stood fast to their proposed principles."[43]

* Results of the Vote may be found in the Appendix.

After the seven sections had been approved, Chase, in a final effort to block action, requested that a vote be taken upon them collectively. President Tyler ruled his request out of order, and the seven provisions of a proposed Amendment XIII of the Constitution went to Congress without the formality of a vote on the document as a whole. Guthrie provided a preamble which delegates approved without a recorded vote.*

Apparently reluctant to adjourn, members began reintroducing old points of controversy. Franklin persisted in proposing a resolution denouncing secession; Coalter moved to delete the entire resolution and substitute an amendment limiting presidents and vice-presidents to six year terms; Seddon substituted a revised version of his scheme for a sectional veto in the Senate. Ruffin then succeeded in getting the whole anticlimactic business laid on the table. A few necessary incidental motions were quickly dispatched; the secrecy rule was removed; and delegates unanimously passed Ewing's motion praising the presiding officer for his dignified and impartial manner. Tyler responded with his usual grandiloquence, invoking "GOD [to] protect our country and the Union of these States, which was committed to us as the blood-bought legacy of our heroic ancestors!" Delegates disagreed even to the sound of the concluding gavel. Five states opposed the motion to adjourn *sine die*.[44]

General Scott ordered a cannonade of one hundred guns to celebrate the termination of the Conference. News of a possible settlement imparted additional buoyancy to the stock market, and there was a well-sustained demand for border-state securities. Now that they had a program around which Union sentiment might crystallize, moderates looked toward a peaceful adjustment.[45] Placing " 'no compromise, no concession' Republicans of the *Tribune* school," in the same treasonable class with the fire-eaters, the Albany *Atlas and Argus* predicted that "disunionists—whether North or South...will be crushed out by the patriotic, Union-loving sentiment of the country." In proclaiming the GLORIOUS RESULT, the Washington *Evening Star* announced, "Every border State has been saved..., and the return of the seceded States to the Union is now but a question of a short time." Convinced that Lincoln had intervened to bring about a settlement, the editor of

* Preamble "To the Congress" may be found in the Appendix.

the *Missouri Republican* saw the way open "for the preservation of the Union as it now exists, and the ultimate restoration of all the States to the confederacy."[46] Radical John M. Forbes of Massachusetts entertained fewer illusions. "So our tremendous Peace Congress has adjourned without either saving or destroying the nation or the world or doing much else than demonstrate to a few respectable Southern gentlemen that we are not all a set of anthropophagi! Yes," he observed cynically to Sumner, "we *did* one thing —talked three weeks & amused the readers of the Tribune. Not such very bad eggs to hatch after all."[47]

## Chapter Ten

# Better Now than Later

Even Scott's cannonading failed to force Congress to give favorable attention to the proposed plan of adjustment. The chaos of the concluding hours of the Thirty-sixth Congress, the excitement of the forthcoming inaugural, and concern over the patronage all combined to divert Northern politicians and the public from giving serious consideration to the seven awkwardly phrased abstractions presented as a Thirteenth Amendment to the Constitution. In his extravagant farewell, President Tyler had promised: "So far as in me lies, therefore, I shall recommend its adoption"; when he transmitted the proposal to Congress, however, he did not take the trouble to enlist his pretentious rhetoric in its support. Eager to return to Richmond, he found time to compose but one prosaic sentence indicating that he was instructed to submit "the accompanying request and proposed amendment." Secretary Puleston hurriedly prepared a letter of transmittal, incorrectly listing Wisconsin as one of the states represented, and implying that *all* delegates approved the proposals submitted.[1]

Because of the previous order of business in the House of Representatives, a two-thirds majority was needed to get the measure received under a suspension of the rules. The papers lay on the Speaker's desk from February 27 to March 1 while sporadic efforts were made to bring the matter up. When John A. McClernand of

Illinois asked for unanimous consent to have the communication read, abolitionist Owen Lovejoy of Illinois objected. Alexander R. Boteler of Virginia wondered how a member could "object to the reception of a communication from the peace congress"; and Lovejoy replied, "It is not a peace congress at all. There is no such body known to this House." There were, he thought, ten thousand things that should take precedence. On March 1, Thaddeus Stevens objected to admitting the propositions "on behalf of John Tyler, who does not want them in. [*Laughter.*]"[2]

After much bickering and parliamentary confusion, McClernand managed to introduce his motion to suspend the rules for the purpose of merely receiving the proposition. Thomas C. Hindman of Arkansas called it unworthy of the vote of any Southern man; Shelton F. Leake of Virginia described it as a miserable abortion; and his colleague, Muscoe R. H. Garnett talked bitterly of "insidious propositions, conceived in fraud and born of cowardice." A few announced that they would support the motion simply for the privilege of voting against the plan of adjustment. When the vote was taken, 93 favored suspension and 67 opposed it; consequently, for want of a two-thirds majority, the House refused even to *receive* the results of the Peace Conference. Radicals voted with the secessionists; moderate Republicans like Thomas Corwin, William Kellogg, and Charles Francis Adams voted with Douglas Democrats, thus encouraging John A. McClernand to announce, "This vote divides the Republican party and sounds its death knell."[3]

When the Peace Conference Amendment was presented in the Senate on February 27, John J. Crittenden succeeded in getting it referred to a select committee of five appointed by the Vice-President: Crittenden, Seward, Trumbull, William Bigler of Pennsylvania, and John R. Thompson of New Jersey. Senator James S. Green of Missouri facetiously suggested that it be referred to the Committee for the District of Columbia; and Senator Jacob Collamer of Vermont recommended "not only that it be made the order of the day for twelve o'clock to-morrow, but that it be adopted by three-fourths of the States the next day. [*Laughter.*]" The select committee endorsed the amendment by a 3 to 2 vote, with Seward and Trumbull submitting a minority report suggesting the possibility of a Convention. "Seward has somewhat betrayed his Richmond Confederates," said the *Virginia Sentinel*. "He led them to suppose that he would do something in the way of conciliating the South. Perhaps he designed to do so; but finding that he could not get his party to follow him, he forfeited his promise and took ground against Crittenden and against the Peace Conference, and fell back on a recommendation to the States to *take into consideration* the *propriety* of holding a National Convention —which is *'nothing* whittled down to a point.' "[4]

Convinced that his own compromise could not pass, and weary from his prolonged effort to secure an adjustment, Crittenden substituted the Peace Conference Amendment for his own during the last hectic hours of the Thirty-sixth Congress. He paid tribute to the great and eminent body of men that convened at Willard's and contended that their proposal offered the "best opportunity for a general concurrence among the States and among the people." Senator James Mason of Virginia emphatically explained why he opposed a substitution which explicitly prohibited slavery north of 36° 30′, but which left Southern rights south of that line to the courts under the common law. Senator Robert W. Johnson of Arkansas called it "a thousand fathoms beneath the propositions of the Senator from Kentucky"; and Green dismissed it as "the merest twaddle that was ever presented to a thinking people." Senator Joseph Lane of Oregon made a long speech urging that the territories be kept "entirely *free* to the enterprise of all," meaning of course free to slavery. His rival, Republican Senator Edward D. Baker, spoke in favor of the Peace Conference Amendment, as did Democratic Senators Stephen A. Douglas and Andrew Johnson. In a vote that came after four o'clock on the morning of March 4, radicals like Bingham, Chandler, Fessenden, Grimes, Sumner, Trumbull, and Wade voted with fire-eaters like Wigfall. Only seven Senators supported the amendment; twenty-eight opposed it. Senator Seward was absent.[5]

When their work was done at Willard's, Southern extremists crossed the Potomac to give support to the Minute-Men. After his concluding speech recommending a spirit of mutual forbearance and concession, Tyler returned to Richmond to labor for secession. At a serenade from the steps of the Exchange Hotel the night after the Conference adjourned, he denounced the proposed plan of adjustment as "a poor, rickety, and disconnected affair," and urged his fellow Virginians to "act promptly and boldly in the exercise of the State sovereignty."[6] Seddon shared the honors with him, proclaiming the amendment "a delusion, a sham, and an offence to the South." Less publicly, but with more spirit, Judge Brockenbrough offered "three gallant boys ready & eager to enlist," claiming: " 'Resistance to tyrants is obedience to God.' "[7]

The proclamations of the Virginia delegates spread dismay among moderates, for as Guthrie said, "If Virginia plays the fool now the whole South is lost to the Union." Rives and Summers attempted to rally Unionist and Conditional Unionist forces, but they got little support from the Old Dominion press. Even the Richmond *Whig* took a "dilly-dally, half & half" position; and the *Enquirer,* of course, attacked submissionists without mercy, accusing them of withholding the real state of affairs at the Peace Conference so as not to "excite the people too much." The proposed amendment was, said the *Enquirer,* "similar in principle and practical application with, and only inferior in candor to, the Chicago platform."[8] A Unionist member of the Virginia Convention, which continued in session, charged that the Negro traders were buying papers "and spending their money freely, in order to influence the public mind in favor of immediate secession." "This City," said S. McDowell Moore, a member from Rockbridge, "is controlled by a Mob, who patrol the streets insulting the Delegates...."[9]

John Janney, moderate chairman of the Convention, begged Crittenden to come to Richmond to aid the conservative cause. Rives prepared a major speech for delivery at Metropolitan Hall in Richmond on March 8. In a point-by-point consideration of the Peace Conference Amendment, he argued that the adjustment was, "as a whole, the most comprehensive and satisfactory settlement...that has yet emanated from any quarter." "The time is gone for the reckless game of precipitation," he concluded. "Our business is to reconcile and reunite North and South, and in the mean time [Virginia should] stand, where nature has placed her, with her sister border slave States." Summers worked to counteract secessionist propaganda in the Convention, where he endorsed Rives' evaluation, claiming the Peace Conference Amendment superior to Crittenden's. Governor Letcher, who heard four hours of his five-hour speech, called it "a hard blow."[10]

Tyler replied the following day with a highly emotional outburst: "When I think of the manner in which all this has been brought about by a race of hungry, artful Catalines, who have misled the Northern mind solely for their own aggrandizement," he declaimed, "my blood becomes so heated in my veins as to scald and burn them in its rapid flow."[11]

In all the border states, moderates and secessionists engaged in the same intense argument. In North Carolina, Unionists needed some conciliatory Republican gesture, for secessionists labored "incessantly," using "all the appliances of deception."[12] Reid, Barringer, and Davis returned from Washington with no illusions of ever achieving a satisfactory settlement. Reporting on his mission in Wilmington, where secession sentiment was increasing, Davis announced that "he could never accept the plan adopted by the 'Peace Congress' as consistent with the rights, the interests or the dignity of North Carolina." She must go with the South or become "the tail-end and victim of a Free Soil North." Reid favored peaceful separation, observing that the conservative element at the North was too weak to control the action of the government.[13] Unionists, of course, were more willing to accept the Peace Conference proposals. "I am satisfied," said one of Ruffin's correspondents, "that the people of the State would pass them all by a majority of six to one. . . ." Morehead, also, thought that the amendment gave "gen[1]. satisfaction," but noted that "our doings . . . undergo various crucifixions by the secessionists. . . ." He quoted Shakespeare to record his own position: ". . . we had better bear the ills we have &c—"[14]

In Tennessee and Kentucky, secessionists advertised the Peace Conference settlement as a disgraceful, free soil measure perpetrated by a body of "venerable dummies." The *Kentucky Statesman* took delight in proclaiming that Republican commissioners refused to yield a syllable of the Chicago creed.[15] James B. Clay endorsed this view and intensified the popular excitement with testimony about "miserable trickery, log-rolling, and clap-trap." Annoyed by such statements, the *Louisville Democrat* accused secessionists of deliberately trying to "get a fight, or keep up the idea that one is coming."[16] But there was, in fact, a widespread fear that failure at the Peace Conference meant an utter disruption of the Union; and even the most hopeful became despondent at reports of Tyler's Exchange Hotel speech. The Nashville *Patriot* urged patience.[17]

Others, however, began to talk of a union of the border states. "I have a poor opinion of Lincoln," said one moderate in a letter to Secessia, "yet I think he is a much better man than many of the leaders of your Cotton Confederacy."[18]

At the Missouri State Convention, Doniphan and Coalter reported that Republican commissioners emasculated the Crittenden Compromise and caviled about everything. Their militant colleague, Waldo P. Johnson, who earlier complained that "leading minds will cling to the Union long after the Constitution has been trampled under foot," issued a report that looked secessionward. The moderate *Missouri Republican* warned Johnson that his constituents opposed extreme opinions and were loyal to the Union under the Constitution. Its editor supported the Peace Conference Amendment and was dismayed to discover that Lincoln had not intervened to bring about its passage, as his paper had announced earlier: "Had ...Lincoln breathed a syllable in [its] favor..., the effect would have been magical in restoring confidence and hope to the country.... But party has prevailed over patriotism and fraternal feeling."[19]

Face-to-face discussion at Willard's proved, at least to the more demanding Conditional Unionists, that no agreeable adjustment could be made with the Northern radicals. No doubt they were more annoyed at radical rhetoric and behavior than with the proposed amendment. "The guarantees recommended...were satisfactory," Reverdy Johnson said, "but the conduct of the Convention, resulting in a great measure from Mr. Field's course, rendered the Convention itself anything but satisfactory."[20] Conditional Unionists came to Washington hopeful of a satisfactory compromise; they left with the bitterness of a suitor scorned. Sentimentally attached to the Union, they courted Northern assurances; rejected, they took up secession with an understandable vigor, intensified by the taunts of those who had warned that it would be so.[21] Thus the moderate Thomas Ruffin of Hillsboro, North Carolina, was eventually driven to counsel, "Fight! Fight! Fight!"[22]

The unconciliatory manner and behavior of radical Congressmen during the debates over the Crittenden Compromise and the summary rejection of the Peace Conference Amendment did even more to encourage secessionist sentiment. Although fire-eaters shared an equal responsibility for defeating these measures in Congress, Southerners generally did not join Rives in condemning them for their share in the defeat.[23] Northern opinion probably did not support the radicals in their militant behavior, but constitutional procedures provided no way in which public sentiment might exert a determining influence until the next scheduled election. Although Crittenden earlier had suggested a popular vote on his proposed amendment, radicals found a referendum challenging their supremacy even more objectionable than the Compromise itself.

Much to the dismay of Southern moderates, Lincoln's inaugural address aided the secessionists. Facing a divided Republican party and a divided North, as well as a divided Union, Lincoln tried primarily to unite his party and, if possible, the entire North in support of an uncompromising policy. Although Seward and Orville H. Browning had persuaded him to modify his address somewhat, it remained, as Weed had predicted, "conciliatory in spirit but nothing more."[24] By refusing to retreat from the Chicago platform, he rallied his radical supporters but alienated still further many Southern moderates. His effective rhetoric translated what Southerners called coercion into a solemn duty to execute "the laws of the Union" "in all the States."[25] Translated into this euphemism, it was a policy all Republicans and perhaps a majority of Northerners could support. Radicals and conservatives alike wrote to congratulate him on his able statement of the issue. Radical Governor John Andrew testified to a "cordial concurrence with the ... policy expressed." Governor Edwin D. Morgan, a moderate, predicted, "It cannot fail to command the confidence of the North and the respect of the South."[26] Both Democrats and Republicans in the Wisconsin Legislature voted to endorse it.[27] Henry J. Raymond concluded in the *New York Times,* "If the Union cannot be saved on this basis and consistently with these principles, then it is better that it should not be saved at all."[28]

Although Southern Unionists discounted secessionist propaganda which called the address a Declaration of War,[29] they nevertheless had hoped for a more conciliatory expression of sentiment.[30] They had begged Lincoln to strengthen their hands in their struggle with old political enemies, the disunionists;[31] they wanted an adjustment on the basis of Crittenden's Compromise—or at least the Peace Conference Amendment—not a promise of what was, to most Southerners regardless of party, coercion. James Guthrie spoke for all Southern moderates when he wrote:

Mr. Lincoln might have prevented all the States but South Carolina from going out by advising his friends in the Senate & the House to go for the Crittenden Constitutional Amendments and he might have saved the border states by saying to his friends in Congress & the Peace Convention to go for the Franklin & Guthrie Constitutional amendments[.] He might have done it by declaring for such in his inaugural. . . .[32]

A devoted old-line Whig, who like Lincoln was an admirer of Henry Clay, pleaded with Crittenden for some word of hope. "I am," said Orlando Brown, "a *National Man,* and hate, from the bottom of my soul, every man who *has been* in any way instrumental in robbing me of my nationality."[33]

With the danger of a compromise averted and the Republicans in control of the federal government, radicals conveniently forgot Chase's slogan, "Inauguration first, adjustment afterward," and agitated for "enforcement of the laws" and "preservation of the Union." In its report to the Legislature, the Empire State delegation denounced the "odious doctrine of property in man": "We do not believe that the people of New York will, under any pressure of circumstances, however grave, recognize a claim so repugnant to humanity, so hostile to freedom." Chittenden concluded that the Conference had served to unite "Republicans and many Democrats in the defense of the Union," and radicals everywhere determined to insure its preservation, "peaceably if they can—forcibly if they must."[34]

———

The Peace Conference strengthened Southern moderates in the February elections in Virginia, North Carolina, Tennessee, and Missouri; it helped to keep all the border states in the Union, thereby enhancing the possibility of Lincoln's peaceable inauguration; it succeeded in presenting a plan of adjustment which a substantial body of opinion supported—perhaps even a majority of voters in those states still in the Union. The proposed amendment offered no solution for sectional economic conflicts, merely constitutional arrangements regarding slavery—and the ultimate hope of solving other disagreements by usual legislative means. Compromise might provide time for passions to subside; it could not restore fraternal feeling.

Northern moderates attempted to rally support for the amendment, but found no constitutional means of effectively registering sentiment in such a crisis. The behavior of the radicals, both in the Peace Conference and in Congress, alienated Conditional Unionist leaders, convincing many of the futility of further negotiation. The subsequent defeat of the proposal by a minority-controlled Congress and Lincoln's uncompromising inaugural intensified this conviction and increased secession sentiment in the border states. Extremists on both sides of the Ohio thus contributed to the failure of a negotiated settlement.

During the debates of the Conference, delegates revealed their ideological rationalizations, if not their economic and political motivations. Sentimental loyalties to the Union and to a common heritage were balanced against conflicting attitudes on slavery, territorial expansion, economic policy, and constitutional interpretation. Slavery provided a convenient symbol for rhetorical manipulation. Though some delegates oversimplified issues, others demonstrated a sophisticated awareness of the clashing economic and psychological forces which eventually led to war. Since their objective was an amendment to the Constitution, delegates spent most of their time debating legal rather than economic matters. The territorial question aroused intense feeling not only because the West was a source of future political power, but because of its vast potential for economic exploitation. Northern Republicans refused to relinquish the economic fruits of political victory: their patronage, their tariff, their expanding industry, their Pacific railroad, their free homesteads—their political future. Southern extremists could not reconcile themselves to the realities of defeat: loss of political power, a circumscribed slave system at the mercy of the elected representatives of an expanding and dynamic Northern industrialism.

The psychological atmosphere was not congenial to a rhetoric of compromise. "We have been defamed by the people of the North," Seddon cried bitterly. "You have educated your children to believe us monsters of brutality, lust and iniquity."[35] In the South, the epithet "Black Republican" aroused the same revolutionary connotations that "anarchist," "bolshevik," and "communist" aroused in succeeding generations, and it was applied with the same lack of discrimination. "The violent men take things by storm," a discerning Tennessee Unionist noted sadly; "the moderate men ... are at once put down by the cry that they are abolitionists, or what is just as bad submissionists."[36] Southerners who supported the Union were thus verbally bludgeoned into silence.

The fatalistic sense of inevitability—the concept of the irrepressible conflict—in itself hastened the day of mobilization. "If the tug has to come," wrote Lincoln in his characteristically rustic metaphor, "better now than later."[37] The less temperate Horace Greeley, speaking for hotheads of every generation, proclaimed in bold type in the *Tribune:* NO NEGOTIATIONS WITH TRAITORS. "Let this intolerable suspense and uncertainty cease!" exclaimed the impetuous Greeley. "If we are to fight, so be it."[38]

Reference
Matter

# List of Delegates

*Maine:* William P. Fessenden, Lot M. Morrill, Daniel E. Somes, John J. Perry, Ezra B. French, Freeman H. Morse, Stephen Coburn, Stephen C. Foster.

*New Hampshire:* Amos Tuck, Levi Chamberlain, Asa Fowler.

*Vermont:* Hiland Hall, Levi Underwood, H. Henry Baxter, Lucius E. Chittenden, Broughton D. Harris.

*Massachusetts:* John Z. Goodrich, Charles Allen, George S. Boutwell, Theophilus P. Chandler, Francis B. Crowninshield, John M. Forbes, Richard P. Waters.

*Rhode Island:* Samuel Ames, Alexander Duncan, William W. Hoppin, George H. Browne, Samuel G. Arnold.

*Connecticut:* Roger S. Baldwin, Chauncey F. Cleveland, Charles J. McCurdy, James T. Pratt, Robbins Battell, Amos S. Treat.

*New York:* David Dudley Field, William Curtis Noyes, James S. Wadsworth, James C. Smith, Amaziah B. James, Erastus Corning, Francis Granger, Greene C. Bronson, William E. Dodge, John A. King, John E. Wool.

*New Jersey:* Charles S. Olden, Peter D. Vroom, Robert F. Stockton, Benjamin Williamson, Joseph F. Randolph, Frederick T. Frelinghuysen, Rodman M. Price, William C. Alexander, Thomas J. Stryker.

*Pennsylvania:* James Pollock, William M. Meredith, David Wilmot, A. W. Loomis, Thomas E. Franklin, William McKennan, Thomas White.

*Delaware:* George B. Rodney, Daniel M. Bates, Henry Ridgely, John W. Houston, William Cannon.

*Maryland:* John F. Dent, Reverdy Johnson, John W. Crisfield, Augustus W. Bradford, William T. Goldsborough, J. Dixon Roman, Benjamin C. Howard.

*Virginia:* John Tyler, William C. Rives, John W. Brockenbrough, George W. Summers, James A. Seddon.

*North Carolina:* George Davis, Thomas Ruffin, David S. Reid, Daniel M. Barringer, John M. Morehead.

*Tennessee:* Samuel Milligan, Josiah M. Anderson, Robert L. Carruthers, Thomas Martin, Isaac R. Hawkins, A. W. O. Totten, Robert J. McKinney, Alvin Cullom, William P. Hickerson, George W. Jones, Felix K. Zollicoffer, William H. Stephens.

*Kentucky:* William O. Butler, James B. Clay, Joshua F. Bell, Charles S. Morehead, James Guthrie, Charles A. Wickliffe.

*Missouri:* John D. Coalter, Alexander W. Doniphan, Waldo P. Johnson, Aylett H. Buckner, Harrison Hough.

*Ohio:* Salmon P. Chase, William S. Groesbeck, Franklin T. Backus, Reuben Hitchcock, Thomas Ewing, Valentine B. Horton, Christopher P. Wolcott, John C. Wright.

*Indiana:* Caleb B. Smith, Pleasant A. Hackleman, Godlove S. Orth, Erastus W. H. Ellis, Thomas C. Slaughter.

*Illinois:* John Wood, Stephen T. Logan, John M. Palmer, Burton C. Cook, Thomas J. Turner.

*Iowa:* James Harlan, James W. Grimes, Samuel R. Curtis, William Vandever.

*Kansas:* Thomas Ewing, Jr., James C. Stone, Henry J. Adams, Martin F. Conway.

# Proposed Amendment XIII to the Constitution of the United States

*To The Congress Of The United States:*

The Convention assembled upon the invitation of the State of Virginia to adjust the unhappy differences which now disturb the peace of the Union and threaten its continuance, make known to the Congress of the United States that their body convened in the city of Washington on the 4th instant, and continued in session until the 27th.

There were in the body, when action was taken upon that which is here submitted, one hundred and thirty-three commissioners, representing the following States: Maine, New Hampshire, Vermont, Massachusetts, Rhode Island, Connecticut, New York, New Jersey, Pennsylvania, Delaware, Maryland, Virginia, North Carolina, Tennessee, Kentucky, Missouri, Ohio, Indiana, Illinois, Iowa, and Kansas.*

They have approved what is herewith submitted, and respectfully request that your honorable body will submit it to conventions in the States as an article of amendment to the Constitution of the United States.

SECTION 1. In all the present territory of the United States north of the parallel of 36° 30′ of north latitude, involuntary servitude, except in punishment of crime, is prohibited. In all the present territory south of that line, the status of persons held to involuntary service or labor, as it now exists, shall not be changed; nor shall any law be passed by Congress or the Territorial Legislature to hinder or prevent the taking of such persons from any of the States of this Union to said territory, nor to impair the rights arising from said relation; but the same shall be subject to judicial cognizance in the Federal courts, according to the course of the common law. When any Territory north or south of said line, within such boundary as Congress may prescribe, shall contain a population equal to that required for a member of Congress, it shall, if its form of government be republican, be admitted into the Union on an equal footing with the original States, with or without involuntary servitude, as the Constitution of such State may provide.

SECTION 2. No territory shall be acquired by the United States, except by discovery, and for naval and commercial stations, depots, and

* Only 132 delegates actually appeared at the Conference. Addison Gardner of New York was nominated as a delegate but did not serve.

transit routes, without the concurrence of a majority of all the Senators from States which allow involuntary servitude, and a majority of all the Senators from States which prohibit that relation; nor shall territory be acquired by treaty, unless the votes of a majority of the Senators from each class of States hereinbefore mentioned be cast as a part of the two-thirds majority necessary to the ratification of such treaty.

SECTION 3. Neither the Constitution nor any amendment thereof shall be construed to give Congress power to regulate, abolish, or control, within any State, the relation established or recognized by the laws thereof touching persons held to labor or involuntary service therein, nor to interfere with or abolish involuntary service in the District of Columbia without the consent of Maryland and without the consent of the owners, or making the owners who do not consent just compensation; nor the power to interfere with or prohibit representatives and others from bringing with them to the District of Columbia, retaining and taking away, persons so held to labor or service; nor the power to interfere with or abolish involuntary service in places under the exclusive jurisdiction of the United States within those States and Territories where the same is established or recognized; nor the power to prohibit the removal or transportation of persons held to labor or involuntary service in any State or Territory of the United States to any other State or Territory thereof, where it is established or recognized by law or usage; and the right during transportation, by sea or river, of touching at ports, shores, and landings, and of landing in case of distress, shall exist; but not the right of transit in or through any State or Territory, or of sale or traffic, against the laws thereof. Nor shall Congress have power to authorize any higher rate of taxation on persons held to labor or service than on land.

The bringing into the District of Columbia of persons held to labor or service for sale, or placing them in depots to be afterwards transferred to other places for sale as merchandise, is prohibited.

SECTION 4. The third paragraph of the second section of the fourth article of the Constitution shall not be construed to prevent any of the States, by appropriate legislation, and through the action of their judicial and ministerial officers, from enforcing the delivery of fugitives from labor to the  person to whom such service or labor is due.

SECTION 5. The foreign slave-trade is hereby forever prohibited; and it shall be the duty of Congress to pass laws to prevent the importation of slaves, coolies, or persons held to service or labor, into the United States and the Territories from places beyond the limits thereof.

SECTION 6. The first, third, and fifth sections, together with this section of these amendments, and the third paragraph of the second section of the first article of the Constitution, and the third paragraph of the second section of the fourth article thereof, shall not be amended or abolished without the consent of all the States.

SECTION 7. Congress shall provide by law that the United States shall pay to the owner the full value of his fugitive from labor, in all cases where the marshal, or other officer, whose duty it was to arrest such fugitive, was prevented from so doing by violence or intimidation from mobs or riotous assemblages, or when, after arrest, such fugitive was rescued by like violence or intimidation, and the owner thereby deprived of the same; and the acceptance of such payment shall preclude the owner from further claim to such fugitive. Congress shall provide by law for securing to the citizens of each State the privileges and immunities of citizens in the several States.

Chittenden, *Report,* pp. 440–49.

## *Results of the Vote*

SECTION 1.

Ayes: Delaware, Illinois, Kentucky, Maryland, New Jersey, Ohio, Pennsylvania, Rhode Island, and Tennessee—9.

Noes: Connecticut, Iowa, Maine, Massachusetts, North Carolina, New Hampshire, Vermont, and Virginia—8.

SECTION 2.

Ayes: Delaware, Indiana, Kentucky, Maryland, Missouri, New Jersey, Ohio, Pennsylvania, Rhode Island, Tennessee, and Virginia—11.

Noes: Connecticut, Illinois, Iowa, Maine, Massachusetts, North Carolina, New Hampshire, and Vermont—8.

SECTION 3.

Ayes: Delaware, Illinois, Kentucky, Maryland, Missouri, New Jersey, North Carolina, Ohio, Pennsylvania, Rhode Island, Tennessee, and Virginia—12.

Noes: Connecticut, Indiana, Iowa, Maine, Massachusetts, New Hampshire, and Vermont—7.

SECTION 4.

Ayes: Connecticut, Delaware, Illinois, Indiana, Kentucky, Maryland, Missouri, New Jersey, North Carolina, Ohio, Pennsylvania, Rhode Island, Tennessee, Vermont, and Virginia—15.

Noes: Iowa, Maine, Massachusetts, and New Hampshire—4.

SECTION 5.

Ayes: Connecticut, Delaware, Illinois, Indiana, Kentucky, Maryland, Missouri, New Jersey, New York, New Hampshire, Ohio, Pennsylvania, Rhode Island, Tennessee, Vermont, and Kansas—16.

Noes: Iowa, Maine, Massachusetts, North Carolina, and Virginia—5.

SECTION 6.

Ayes: Delaware, Illinois, Kentucky, Maryland, Missouri, New Jersey, Ohio, Pennsylvania, Rhode Island, Tennessee, and Kansas—11.

Noes: Connecticut, Indiana, Iowa, Maine, Massachusetts, North Carolina, New Hampshire, Vermont, and Virginia—9.

SECTION 7.

Ayes: Delaware, Illinois, Indiana, Kentucky, Maryland, New Jersey, New Hampshire, Ohio, Pennsylvania, Rhode Island, Tennessee, and Kansas—12.

Noes: Connecticut, Iowa, Maine, Missouri, North Carolina, Vermont, and Virginia—7.

Chittenden, *Report,* pp. 441–45.

## CHAPTER ONE

1 Washington *Evening Star,* February 2 and 5, 1861; William H. Seward, Washington, to E. D. Morgan, February 14, 1861, Morgan MSS.

2 Springfield *Weekly Illinois State Journal,* February 6, 1861; Washington *Evening Star,* February 5, 1861.

3 Washington *Evening Star,* February 4, 5, and 16, 1861; Albert G. Riddle, *Recollections of War Times: Reminiscences of Men and Events in Washington, 1860–1865* (New York, 1895), p. 8.

4 Washington *Evening Star,* February 4, 5, 13, and 14, 1861; *New York Times,* February 1 and 5, 1861.

5 Washington *Evening Star,* February 4 and 5, 1861.

6 C. F. Adams, Washington, to John A. Andrew, February 8, 1861, Andrew MSS-1. The conservative Republican *Times* thought the Adams *"enabling act for New Mexico"* "the proper remedy for all existing evils."—*New York Times,* February 28, 1861. Radicals, on the other hand, "worked night and day to defeat all Compromises."—John A. Gilmer, Washington, to D. H. Albright, January 8, 1861 [misdated 1860], Gilmer MSS.

7 T. P. Chandler, Brookline, Mass., to John A. Andrew, January 6, 1861, Andrew MSS-1; William Hebard and others, Montpelier, Vt., to Justin S. Morrill, February 5, 1861, Justin S. Morrill MSS; William Lloyd Garrison to Lydia Mott [January, 1861], HM 10524, Henry E. Huntington Library.

8   George D. Morgan to E. D. Morgan, January 12, 1861, Morgan MSS. See also Robert G. Gunderson, "Lincoln and Governor Morgan: A Financial Footnote," *The Abraham Lincoln Quarterly,* VI (December, 1951), 431–37.

9   Madison *Argus & Democrat,* January 29, 1861; Washington *Evening Star,* February 4, 1861.

10   *Acts of the General Assembly of the State of Virginia Passed in 1861* (Richmond, 1861), pp. 337–39.

11   Washington *Evening Star,* February 4 and 14, 1861.

12   John M. Palmer, Washington, to John M. Palmer, Jr., February 10, 1861, Palmer MSS; Mrs. Lyman Trumbull, Washington, to Walter Trumbull, January 26, 1861, in Horace White, *The Life of Lyman Trumbull* (Boston, 1913), pp. 121–22.

13   Chittenden, MS Address; see also Lucius E. Chittenden, *Recollections of President Lincoln and His Administration* (New York, 1891), pp. 21–22.

14   Sarah Forbes Hughes (ed.), *Letters and Recollections of John Murray Forbes* (2 vols., Boston, 1900), I, 188, 190.

15   Mrs. John Tyler, Washington, to Mrs. David Gardiner, February 13, 1861, in Lyon G. Tyler, *The Letters and Times of the Tylers* (3 vols., Richmond, 1884–96), II, 613.

16   Henry Adams, Washington, to Charles Francis Adams, Jr., December 29, 1860, and January 11, 1861, in Worthington C. Ford (ed.), *Letters of Henry Adams, 1858–1891* (Boston, 1930), pp. 74–75, 79.

17   [William H. Seward], Washington, to Abraham Lincoln, December 29, 1860, R. T. Lincoln Collection; Horace Greeley, New York, to William H. Herndon, December 26, 1860, *ibid.;* David Hunter, Fort Leavenworth, to Abraham Lincoln, December 18, 1860, *ibid.*

18   J. Medill, Washington, to Abraham Lincoln, December 31, 1860, *ibid.*

19   E. B. Washburne, Washington, to Abraham Lincoln, February 3, 1861, *ibid.;* Charles Sumner [quoting Stanton], Senate Chamber, to John Andrew, January 28, 1861, Andrew MSS-1.

20   Curtis, MS Journal; E. B. Washburne, House of Reps., to Abraham Lincoln, January 30 and February 3, 1861, R. T. Lincoln Collection; Winfield Scott, Washington, to E. D. Morgan, January 17, 1861, Morgan MSS.

21   Washington *Evening Star,* January 24, 25, 30, and February 2 and 4, 1861; Madison *Argus & Democrat,* February 14, 1861; *Detroit Free Press,* January 27 and February 7, 1861.

22   Simon Cameron, [Washington], to Abraham Lincoln, January 3, 1861 [misdated 1860], R. T. Lincoln Collection; Washington

*Evening Star,* January 31 and February 19, 1861; *Detroit Free Press,* January 27 and February 5, 1861; *Chicago Tribune,* February 13, 1861, quoted in Madison *Wisconsin State Journal,* February 18, 1861; *New York Semi-Weekly Tribune,* February 22, 1861.

23  Washington *Evening Star,* February 4, 1861.

24  *Ibid.,* January 24, 29, 30, February 6 and 7, 1861; *Detroit Free Press,* February 12, 1861.

25  Washington *Constitution,* n.d., quoted in Washington *Evening Star,* January 30, 1861; Baltimore *American,* n.d., quoted *ibid.,* February 1, 1861.

26  Washington *Evening Star,* January 31, 1861; John Tyler, Washington, to Governor John Letcher, January 27, 1861, in Philip G. Auchampaugh, *Robert Tyler, Southern Rights Champion* (Duluth, 1934), p. 323.

27  Washington correspondence, February 6, 1861, in *Detroit Free Press,* February 12, 1861; Chittenden, *Recollections of Lincoln,* p. 20; Hughes (ed.), *Letters of John M. Forbes,* I, 197–98.

28  Chittenden, MS Address.

29  Washington *Evening Star,* February 11, 1861.

30  Mrs. John Tyler, Washington, to Mrs. David Gardiner, February 3 and 4, 1861, in Tyler, *Letters,* II, 596–97; St. Louis *Missouri Republican,* February 9, 1861; *Louisville Democrat,* February 10, 1861; Connelsville [*sic*], *Patriot* (Ohio), February 8, 1861, quoted in *New York Semi-Weekly Tribune,* February 15, 1861; George Thomas Palmer, *A Conscientious Turncoat, the Story of John M. Palmer* (New Haven, 1941), p. 60.

31  Warrenton *Flag of '98,* February 14, 1861.

32  Robert G. Gunderson, "John C. Wright and 'the Old Gentlemen's Convention,'" in Historical and Philosophical Society of Ohio *Bulletin,* XII (April, 1954), 109–18.

33  Lucius E. Chittenden, *A Report of the Debates and Proceedings in the Secret Sessions of the Conference Convention, for Proposing Amendments to the Constitution of the United States Held at Washington, D.C., in February, A.D. 1861* (New York, 1864), p. 314.

34  William C. Rives, Castle Hill, [Va.], to Alexander R. Boteler, December 8, 1860, HM 23783, Henry E. Huntington Library.

35  John G. Nicolay and John Hay, *Abraham Lincoln: A History* (10 vols., New York, 1904), IX, 100.

36  Allen Johnson, Dumas Malone, and Harris E. Starr (eds.), *Dictionary of American Biography* (21 vols. and index, New York, 1928–44), XI, 365–66.

37 Mrs. John Tyler, Washington, to Mrs. David Gardiner, February 13, 1861, in Tyler, *Letters,* II, 612.
38 *Dictionary of American Biography,* XVI, 545–46.
39 *New York Semi-Weekly Tribune,* February 1 and 8, 1861; New Orleans *Bee,* February 14, 1861, quoted in Dwight L. Dumond (ed.), *Southern Editorials on Secession* (New York, 1931), p. 456; *Cincinnati Enquirer,* February 13, 1861.

CHAPTER TWO

1 Thomas Corwin, Washington, to Abraham Lincoln, January 18, 1861, R. T. Lincoln Collection.
2 Carl Schurz, Manchester, N.H., to Abraham Lincoln, December 18, 1860, *ibid.*
3 Elizur Wright, Boston, to Charles Sumner, January 19, 1861, Sumner MSS.
4 E. L. Pierce [quoting a letter from Horace White], Boston, to Charles Sumner, January 3, 1861, *ibid.*
5 Albany *Atlas & Argus,* February 19, 1861.
6 Montgomery *Mail,* n.d., quoted in *New York Times,* November 1, 1860; Henry A. Wise to Committee at Madison Court House, Virginia, November 19, 1860, in *New York Semi-Weekly Tribune,* November 30, 1860; Charleston *Mercury,* n.d., quoted in *New York Semi-Weekly Tribune,* October 23, 1860.
7 *New York Semi-Weekly Tribune,* November 13, 20, and 23, 1860; *Hartford Times,* November 19, 1860, quoted *ibid.,* November 23, 1860; *New York Times,* January 11, 1861; Washington *National Intelligencer,* February 28, 1861; J. G. Randall, *The Civil War and Reconstruction* (New York, 1937), p. 233.
8 A. Mordecai, Watervliet Arsenal, to G. W. Mordecai, January 20, 1861, Mordecai MSS; John W. Ellis, [Raleigh], to Robert N. Gourdin, December [16?, 1860], copy in Ellis, MS Letterbook.
9 John W. Ellis, Raleigh, to I. W. Garrott, January 30, 1861, copy in Ellis, MS Letterbook.
10 Washington *Evening Star,* February 7, 1861; J. G. de Roulhac Hamilton, *Reconstruction in North Carolina* (Raleigh, 1906), pp. 19–20.
11 MS Acts of the Virginia General Assembly, January 10 and 25, 1861, Virginia State Library, Richmond; Alexander Jones, New York, to John Letcher, January 10, 12 and 30, 1861; L. S. [?]

Harris, n.p., to John Letcher, January 8, 1861, Letcher, Executive Papers.

12  J. D. Davidson, Lexington, Va., to William C. Rives, February 1, 1861, William C. Rives MSS.

13  *New York Semi-Weekly Tribune,* November 27, 1860.

14  Former South Carolina Governor James H. Adams, *ibid.,* December 14, 1860.

15  *Ibid.,* December 4, 1860.

16  *Ibid.,* December 11, 1860. For a discussion of these resignations, see Philip G. Auchampaugh, *James Buchanan and His Cabinet on the Eve of Secession* (Lancaster, Pa., 1926).

17  Raleigh *State Journal,* December 26, 1860, quoted in J. Carlyle Sitterson, *The Secession Movement in North Carolina* (Chapel Hill, 1939), p. 187.

18  *New York Semi-Weekly Tribune,* December 14, 1860; *New York Times,* November 23, 1860.

19  Toombs quoted in George Fort Milton, *The Eve of Conflict: Stephen A. Douglas and the Needless War* (Boston, 1934), p. 504.

20  *New York Semi-Weekly Tribune,* November 9, 1860.

21  *New York Times,* December 1, 1860.

22  *New York Semi-Weekly Tribune,* November 23, December 4 and 7, 1860.

23  *New York Times,* December 1 and 17, 1860; *New York Semi-Weekly Tribune,* December 14 and 18, 1860; *Louisville Journal,* February 11, 1861.

24  William S. Speer, Shelbyville, Tenn., to Lyman Trumbull, January 16, 1861, Trumbull MSS.

25  Horace White, Chicago, to Lyman Trumbull, December 30, 1860, *ibid.*

26  *New York Times,* December 25, 1860. Though the Congressmen talked expansively, the total personnel of the army at this time was approximately 16,000. Fred A. Shannon, *The Organization and Administration of the Union Army, 1861–1865* (2 vols., Cleveland, 1928), I, 27.

27  M. B. Anderson, Rochester, N.Y., to Thurlow Weed, February 8, 1861, Weed Collection; E. B. Washburne, Washington, to Abraham Lincoln, February 3, 1861, R. T. Lincoln Collection.

28  J. R. Doolittle, Washington, to Abraham Lincoln, January 10, 1861, R. T. Lincoln Collection.

29  Charles Sumner, Senate Chamber, to John A. Andrew, January 21, 1861, Andrew MSS-1.

30  Everett, MS Diary, Tuesday, January 29, 1861.

31   Thurlow Weed, Albany, to Abraham Lincoln, January 10, 1861, R. T. Lincoln Collection.

32   Henry Adams, Washington, to Charles Francis Adams, Jr., January 11 and 17, 1861, in Worthington C. Ford (ed.), *Letters of Henry Adams, 1858–1891* (Boston, 1930), pp. 74–75, 79.

33   T. P. Chandler, Brookline, Mass., to John Andrew, January 6, 1861, Andrew MSS-1.

34   Lyman Trumbull, Washington, to Abraham Lincoln, December 24, 1860, R. T. Lincoln Collection.

35   P. W. Curtenius, Kalamazoo, to Abraham Lincoln, December 31, 1860, and Edwin C. Wilson, Erie, Pa., to Abraham Lincoln, January 30, 1861, *ibid.*

36   Erastus Fairbanks, St. Johnsbury, Vt., to John Andrew, January 7, 1861, Andrew MSS-1; Erastus Fairbanks, St. Johnsbury, to E. D. Morgan, January 7, 1861, Morgan MSS.

37   E. D. Morgan, Albany, to General Winfield Scott, January 15, 1861, and E. D. Morgan, Albany, to Preston King, January 26, 1861, copies in Morgan, MS Letterbook; John M. Forbes to John Andrew, February 2, 1861, Andrew MSS-1. Forbes gives a survey of available ships with an estimate of their capacity to transport troops to Baltimore and Washington.

38   T. S. Mather, Washington, to Richard Yates, Confidential, January 29, 1861, Yates MSS. Mather was sent as an agent of Governor Yates to General Scott on a mission to obtain arms. Winfield Scott, Washington, to E. D. Morgan, January 17, 1861, and William H. Seward, Washington, to E. D. Morgan, February 11, 1861, Morgan MSS; E. D. Morgan, Albany, to Thurlow Weed, February 7, 1861, Weed Collection.

39   Allen C. Fuller, Belvidere, Ill., to Richard Yates, December 30, 1860, and J. Young Scammon, Chicago, to Richard Yates, December 27, 1860, Yates MSS; Horace White, Chicago, to Lyman Trumbull, December 30, 1860, Trumbull MSS.

40   J. Medill, Washington, to Abraham Lincoln, December 26, 1860, R. T. Lincoln Collection.

41   E. B. Washburne, Washington, to Charles Henry Ray, January 13, 1861, Ray MSS.

42   Richard Yates, Springfield, Ill., to Lyman Trumbull, January 22, 1861, Trumbull MSS; T. S. Mather, Washington, to Richard Yates, January 29, 1861, Yates MSS; Edward Bates, St. Louis, to Abraham Lincoln, January 30, 1861, R. T. Lincoln Collection.

43   Kenneth M. Stampp, *Indiana Politics during the Civil War* (Indianapolis, 1949), pp. 66–70.

44 Carl Schurz, Keene, N.H., to Abraham Lincoln, December 28, 1860, R. T. Lincoln Collection.

45 David Hunter, Fort Leavenworth, to Lincoln, December 18, 1860, *ibid.*

46 George P. Bissel, Hartford, to Abraham Lincoln, December 30, 1860, and Jerome B. Wass, New York, to Abraham Lincoln, February 25, 1861, *ibid.*

47 E. B. Pomeroy, Lafayette, Ill., to Lyman Trumbull, February 5, 1861, Trumbull MSS.

48 *New York Semi-Weekly Tribune,* November 9, 1860, and February 12, 1861; Horace Greeley, New York, to Abraham Lincoln, December 22, 1860, R. T. Lincoln Collection.

49 Salmon P. Chase, Columbus, to Abraham Lincoln, January 28, 1861, R. T. Lincoln Collection.

50 J. D. Webster, Chicago, to Lyman Trumbull, February 7, 1861, Trumbull MSS.

51 Madison *Wisconsin State Journal,* February 6, 1861, quoted in *New York Semi-Weekly Tribune,* February 15, 1861.

52 Henry Asbury, Quincy, Ill., to Lyman Trumbull, February 10, 1861, Trumbull MSS.

53 Danville *Vermillion County Press* (Illinois), February 6, 1861, quoted in *New York Semi-Weekly Tribune,* February 15, 1861.

54 Joseph Medill, Washington, to Charles Henry Ray, Confidential, January 13, 1861, Ray MSS.

55 William H. Seward, Washington, to Abraham Lincoln, January 27, 1861, R. T. Lincoln Collection.

56 James Dixon, Washington, to Gideon Welles, January 27, 1861, Wells MSS-2.

57 William H. Herndon, Springfield, Ill., to Lyman Trumbull, January 27, 1861, Trumbull MSS.

58 JPR [Mrs. William C. Rives], Castle Hill, to ———— [her son], January 21, 1861, Alfred Landon Rives MSS.

59 *New York Semi-Weekly Tribune,* February 8, 1861; Abraham Lincoln, Springfield, Ill., to William H. Seward, February 1, 1861, in Roy P. Basler (ed.), *The Collected Works of Abraham Lincoln* (8 vols, and index, New Brunswick, N.J.), IV, 183; William Jayne, Springfield, Ill., to Lyman Trumbull, January 28, 1861, Trumbull MSS.

60 Carl Schurz, Springfield, Ill., "an seine Frau," February 9, 1861, Schurz MSS.

61 Salmon P. Chase, Columbus, to Abraham Lincoln, January 28, 1861, R. T. Lincoln Collection.

62   See letters to Lyman Trumbull during January and February, 1861, Trumbull MSS.

63   Springfield *Illinois State Journal,* March 27, 1861.

64   Charleston, S.C., correspondence, December 7, 1860, in *New York Semi-Weekly Tribune,* December 14, 1860; L. A. to Major Robert Anderson, "Received, January 24, 1861," quoted in Auchampaugh, *Buchanan and His Cabinet,* p. 184; *Louisville Democrat,* March 3, 1861.

65   J. R. Giddings, Jefferson, Ohio, to G. W. Julian, December 14, 1860, Giddings-Julian Collection.

66   [J. P.] Allyn to Gideon Welles, [January 12, 1861], Welles MSS-2.

67   C. C. Chaffee, Washington, to John Andrew, February 4, 1861, Andrew MSS-1.

68   S. A. Douglas to "a newspaper in Tennessee," February 2, 1861, quoted in J. Thomas Scharf, *History of Maryland* (Baltimore, 1879), p. 378.

69   C. Davisson, St. Louis, to Lyman Trumbull, December 25, 1860, Trumbull MSS; John W. Ellis, Raleigh, to Robert N. Gourdin, December [16, 1860], copy in Ellis, MS Letterbook; *Louisville Journal,* February 11, 1861.

70   Charlotte *Bulletin* (N.C.), n.d., quoted in Sitterson, *Secession Movement in North Carolina,* p. 201.

71   J. A. Kennedy, New York, to E. D. Morgan, January 13, 1861, Morgan MSS.

72   Albany *Atlas & Argus,* February 18, 1861.


CHAPTER THREE

1   *Louisville Journal,* August 14, 1860, quoted in Mary Scrugham, *The Peaceable Americans of 1860–1861: A Study in Public Opinion* (New York, 1921), p. 16; *Louisville Democrat,* February 21, 1861.

2   Washington *Evening Star,* February 18, 1861.

3   Oliver P. Chitwood, *John Tyler, Champion of the Old South* (New York, 1939), p. 439; J. G. Randall, *The Civil War and Reconstruction* (New York, 1937), p. 199; William C. Rives, Castle Hill, to Alexander R. Boteler, December 8, 1860, HM 23783, Henry E. Huntington Library.

4   S. Draper to Thurlow Weed, December 17, 1860, Weed Collection; Louisville correspondence, December 27, 1860, in *New York*

*Times,* January 7, 1861; Lucius E. Chittenden, *A Report of the Debates and Proceedings in the Secret Sessions of the Conference Convention, for Proposing Amendments to the Constitution of the United States Held at Washington, D.C., in February, A.D. 1861* (New York, 1864), pp. 62–63; *Kentucky House Journal, January, 1861* (Frankfort, 1861), pp. 9, 133–35, 137–40.

5   *Tennessee Senate Journal, January, 1861* (Nashville, 1861), pp. 97–103; Chittenden, *Report,* pp. 454–55.

6   Lyon G. Tyler, *The Letters and Times of the Tylers* (3 vols., Richmond, 1884–96), II, 579; John Tyler, Sherwood Forest, to Caleb Cushing, December 14, 1860, in *ibid.,* II, 577; *Richmond Enquirer,* January 17, 1861.

7   Henry A. Wise, *Seven Decades of the Union* (Philadelphia, 1872), p. 271; Letcher, Executive Papers; E. B. Prettyman, "John Letcher," in *The John P. Branch Historical Papers of Randolph-Macon College* (Richmond, Virginia, 1912), III, 337–39.

8   Washington *Evening Star,* January 23, 1861; Tyler, *Letters,* II, 580; Henry T. Shanks, *The Secession Movement in Virginia, 1847–1861* (Richmond, Virginia, 1934), p. 253. It has been suggested that William H. Seward may have "initiated" the Peace Conference since he was in communication with Barbour. Though he may in fact have given encouragement to the proposal, the New York Senator can hardly be credited with causing the "Convention to be summoned," as Henry Adams claimed.—Henry Adams, "The Great Secession Winter of 1860–61," *Proceedings of the Massachusetts Historical Society, October, 1909—June, 1910* (Boston, 1910), XLIII, 680; David M. Potter, *Lincoln and His Party in the Secession Crisis* (New Haven, 1942), pp. 308–9.

9   *Journal of the House of Delegates of the State of Virginia for the Extra Session, 1861* (Richmond, 1861), pp. 65–67; *Acts of the General Assembly of the State of Virginia Passed in 1861* (Richmond, 1861), pp. 337–39.

10   A. L. Caperton, Richmond, to William C. Rives, February 3, 1861, William C. Rives MSS.

11   Tyler, *Letters,* II, 581; *Richmond Enquirer,* January 23, 1861; *Louisville Journal,* February 1, 1861.

12   *New York Times,* November 9, 1860.

13   *New York Semi-Weekly Tribune,* February 8 and 12, 1861.

14   George D. Morgan, New York, to E. D. Morgan, February 1, 1861, Morgan MSS; Lyman Trumbull, Washington, to Abraham Lincoln, December 14, 1860, R. T. Lincoln Collection; Washington *Evening Star,* February 18, 1861.

15  *New York Times,* December 4, 7, and 15, 1860; January 11 and February 1, 1861.

16  E. D. Morgan, Albany, to Abraham Lincoln, December 16, 1860, R. T. Lincoln Collection; *New York Times,* December 26, 1860; George D. Morgan to E. D. Morgan, January 12, 1861, Morgan MSS.

17  Samuel A. Pleasants, *Fernando Wood of New York* (New York, 1948), p. 114.

18  J. F. Potter, East Troy, Wis., to James R. Doolittle, October 3, 1860, Doolittle MSS-2.

19  Hamilton Fish, New York, to William P. Fessenden, December 11, 1860, Fessenden MSS.

20  M. H. Grinnell, J. J. Astor, Jr., R. M. Blatchford, Hamilton Fish, James A. Hamilton, George D. Morgan, R. B. Minturn, and others, New York, to Abraham Lincoln, January 29, 1861, R. T. Lincoln Collection.

21  A. T. Stewart, New York, to Thurlow Weed, February 20, 1861, Weed Collection; George D. Morgan, New York, to E. D. Morgan, January 22, 1861, Morgan MSS. Philip Foner examines the relationships between business and slavery in great detail.— Philip S. Foner, *Business & Slavery, The New York Merchants and the Irrepressible Conflict* (Chapel Hill, 1941).

22  *New York Times,* December 4, 1861; Poughkeepsie *Eagle,* February 12, 1861, quoted in *New York Semi-Weekly Tribune,* February 15, 1861.

23  W. C. Bryant, New York, to Abraham Lincoln, December 25, 1861, R. T. Lincoln Collection.

24  Thurlow Weed, New York, to Leonard Swett, January 20, 1861, R. T. Lincoln Collection; Carl Schurz, Boston, to J. F. Potter, December 24, 1860, in Frederic Bancroft (ed.), *Speeches, Correspondence and Political Papers of Carl Schurz* (6 vols., New York, 1913), I, 173–74.

25  Weed's conservative friends demonstrated their strength by defeating Horace Greeley in a bitter battle for the U.S. Senatorship in February, 1861. "We have," said Weed, "after a desperate struggle with all the Radicals against us . . . paid the first instalment in a large debt to Mr. Greeley."—T. Weed, Albany, to A. C. Wildar, February 3, 1861, Weed Collection.

26  [J. P.] Allyn to Gideon Welles, [January 12, 1861?], Welles MSS-2.

27  *Detroit Free Press,* February 1, 1861; James Dixon, Washington, to Gideon Welles, January 29, 1861, Welles MSS-2.

28  Curtis, MS Journal, February 1, 1861.

29  James D. Ogden, New York, to John C. Crittenden, January 12,

1861, Crittenden MSS; Nat Vose to E. B. Washburne, January 27, 1861, E. B. Washburne MSS; *New York Semi-Weekly Tribune,* February 5, 1861.

30 Everett, MS Diary, January 21 to 29, 1861; *Detroit Free Press,* February 23, 1861; *Boston Evening Transcript,* February 4, 1861.

31 *New York Times,* February 15, 1861; *Detroit Free Press,* February 12, 1861; *New York Semi-Weekly Tribune,* February 15, 1861; George Morey, Boston, to William Pitt Fessenden, January 12, 1861, Fessenden MSS.

32 Stephen A. Douglas, Washington, to Rev. W. S. Prentice, December 5, 1860, Douglas MSS; John Bell to A. Burwell, [December 6, 1860], in the *New York Semi-Weekly Tribune,* December 14, 1860; William B. Hesseltine, *The South in American History* (New York, 1943), pp. 373–74; Randall, *Civil War and Reconstruction,* pp. 182–83.

33 G. H. Shirly, New York, to John J. Crittenden, January 17, 1861, Crittenden MSS.

34 A. L. Kohlmeier, *The Old Northwest ... A Study in Commerce and Politics* (Bloomington, Indiana, 1938), pp. 211–14. Another writer disagrees with the emphasis placed upon this commerce, but nevertheless admits that the "Southern trade was still profoundly important in 1860."—Charles R. Wilson, "Cincinnati, a Southern Outpost in 1860–1861," *Mississippi Valley Historical Review,* XXIV (March, 1938), 473–82.

35 Edward Bates, St. Louis, to Samuel Bulkley Ruggles, January 7, 1861, HM 23362, Henry E. Huntington Library; Lucian Barbour, Indianapolis, to Lyman Trumbull, January 18, 1861, Trumbull MSS.

36 New Albany *Weekly Ledger* (Indiana), August 20, 1856, quoted in Kenneth M. Stampp, *Indiana Politics during the Civil War* (Indianapolis, 1949), p. 12.

37 Stampp, *Indiana Politics during the Civil War,* pp. 52–54.

38 *Louisville Democrat,* February 3, 1861.

39 *New York Times,* November 12, 23, and 29, 1860.

40 *Louisville Democrat,* n.d., quoted *ibid.,* November 17, 1860.

41 *New York Times,* November 28, 1860.

42 *Ibid.,* January 10, 1861; Washington *National Intelligencer,* January 29, 1861; Kenneth Rayner, Raleigh, to Thomas Ruffin, December 25, 1860, in J. G. de Roulhac Hamilton (ed.), *The Papers of Thomas Ruffin* (4 vols., Raleigh, 1918–20), III, 109; F. P. Blair, Sr., Silver Springs, Md., to Abraham Lincoln, January 14, 1861, R. T. Lincoln Collection.

43 *Louisville Democrat,* February 16, 1861; St. Louis *Missouri*

*Statesman,* n.d., quoted in *New York Semi-Weekly Tribune,* November 20, 1860.

44  Raleigh *North Carolina Standard,* February 5, 1861, quoted in J. Carlyle Sitterson, *The Secession Movement in North Carolina* (Chapel Hill, 1939).

45  *Louisville Journal,* February 11, 1861.

46  Emerson Etheridge, Washington, to Richard Yates, January 14, 1861, Yates MSS; Thurlow Weed Barnes, *Memoir of Thurlow Weed* (Boston, 1884), p. 316.

47  Thurlow Weed, Washington, to E. D. Morgan, February 11, 1861, Morgan MSS; William H. Seward to Abraham Lincoln, January 27, 1861, R. T. Lincoln Collection.

48  W. C. Kyle, Rogersville, Tenn., to T. A. R. Nelson, February 6, 1861, and A. A. Kyle, Rogersville, Tenn., to Nelson, February 19, 1861, Nelson MSS.


CHAPTER FOUR

1  William Dennison, Columbus, to Richard Yates, telegram, January 26, 1861, R. T. Lincoln Collection; William Dennison, Columbus, to E. D. Morgan, telegram, January 26, 1861, Morgan MSS; O. P. Morton, Indianapolis, to William Dennison, January 25, 1861, Dennison MSS; Israel Washburn, Augusta, Me., to John A. Andrew, January 31, 1861, Andrew MSS-1; *New York Times,* February 5, 1861.

2  O. P. Morton, Indianapolis, to Richard Yates, telegram, January 25, 1861, and O. P. Morton, Indianapolis, to Abraham Lincoln, January 29, 1861, R. T. Lincoln Collection.

3  Thurlow Weed, Albany, to Abraham Lincoln, January 28, 1861, *ibid.*

4  Springfield *Weekly Illinois State Journal,* January 30, 1861; N. B. Judd, Springfield, Ill., to Salmon P. Chase, January 11, 1861, Chase MSS-1; William Jayne, Springfield, Ill., to Lyman Trumbull, January 18, 1861, Trumbull MSS; William Jayne, Springfield, Ill., to Lyman Trumbull, January 28, 1861; Lincoln's opposition is also indicated in E. Peck, Springfield, Ill., to Lyman Trumbull, February 2, 1861, *ibid.*

5  William Jayne, Springfield, Ill., to Lyman Trumbull, January 31, 1861, *ibid.* Other less reliable testimony indicated that only "the very active intervention" of Bates was sufficient "to overcome the [Radical] prejudice."—[J. C. ?] Chrisman, Galesburg, Ill., to William C. Rives, February 4, 1861, William C. Rives MSS.

6 E. Peck, Springfield, Ill., to Lyman Trumbull, February 2, 1861, Trumbull MSS. Peck's reasoning is confirmed by W. Jayne, Springfield, Ill., to Lyman Trumbull, February 1, 1861, *ibid.;* and by J. N. Jones, Springfield, Ill., to Elihu B. Washburne, February 1 and 3, 1861, E. B. Washburne MSS.

7 G. Koerner, Springfield, Ill., to Lyman Trumbull, February 19, 1861, Trumbull MSS; *New York Times,* February 4, 1861; Jesse K. Dubois and William Butler to Abraham Lincoln, n.d., with penciled reply, signed "A. Lincoln," Abraham Lincoln MSS-2.

8 *Illinois Senate Journal, 1861* (Springfield, 1861), p. 231; Springfield *Weekly Illinois State Journal,* February 6, 1861.

9 Robert Dale Owen, Indianapolis, to John Tyler, February 14, 1861, Tyler MSS-1.

10 C. M. Allen, Indiana Hall House Reps., to Abraham Lincoln, January 25, 1861, R. T. Lincoln Collection; O. P. Morton, Indianapolis, to Abraham Lincoln, January 29, 1861, *ibid.*

11 O. P. Morton, Indianapolis, to Commissioners to Washington, February 1, 1861; P. A. Hackleman, Indianapolis, to O. P. Morton, February 1, 1861, Morton MSS; William Dudley Foulke, *Life of Oliver P. Morton* (2 vols., Indianapolis, 1899), I, 105; *Indiana House Journal, 1861* (Indianapolis, 1861), p. 278; *Indiana Senate Journal, 1861* (Indianapolis, 1861), p. 222; Kenneth M. Stampp, "Letters from the Washington Peace Conference of 1861," *The Journal of Southern History,* IX (August, 1943), 394–403.

12 Robert G. Gunderson, "Letters from the Washington Peace Conference of 1861," *The Journal of Southern History,* XVII (August, 1951), 382–92.

13 J. D. Cox, Warren, Ohio, to Ben Wade, December 21, 1860, Wade MSS; Johnson H. Jordan, Cincinnati, to Lyman Trumbull, February 26, 1861, Trumbull MSS; William Dennison, Columbus, to Richard Yates, telegram, January 26, 1861, R. T. Lincoln Collection.

14 *Ohio House Journal, 1861* (Columbus, 1861), pp. 102–12; *Ohio Senate Journal, 1861* (Columbus, 1861), pp. 50, 57–59; *New York Times,* January 31 and February 1, 1861.

15 *Cincinnati Enquirer,* January 31 and February 1, 1861; W. S. Groesbeck, Cincinnati, to William Dennison, February 1, 1861, Dennison MSS; Salmon P. Chase, Columbus, to Joshua R. Giddings, February 1, 1861, Giddings MSS.

16 *New York Assembly Journal, 1861* (Albany, 1861), p. 157; James A. Hamilton, Dobbs Ferry, to E. D. Morgan, January 26, 1861, Morgan MSS; Frederic Bancroft, *The Life of William H. Seward* (New York, 1900), II, 18.

17   B. F. Manierre, Senate Chamber, Albany, to Charles Sumner, January 29, 1861, Sumner MSS.

18   Each issue of the *Tribune* in February reprinted anticompromise editorials under this heading; *New York Times,* January 31, 1861.

19   *New York Senate Journal, 1861* (Albany, 1861), pp. 127, 134, 139–44; *New York Assembly Journal, 1861,* pp. 158–59, 166–79, 205, 225–27, 256–61, 283, 295; *New York Times,* February 11, 1861; Albany *Atlas & Argus,* March 4, 1861.

20   *New York Semi-Weekly Tribune,* February 26, 1861; John L. O'Neal, Philadelphia, to John J. Crittenden, January 25, 1861, Crittenden MSS; Washington *Evening Star,* January 23, 1861.

21   *Pennsylvania Senate Journal, 1861* (Harrisburg, 1861), pp. 141, 147, 151, 165, 175, 212; *Pennsylvania House Journal, 1861* (Harrisburg, 1861), pp. 152, 178, 193, 195–200, 266; *New York Semi-Weekly Tribune,* February 15, 1861; Stanton Ling Davis, *Pennsylvania Politics, 1860–1863* (Cleveland, 1935), pp. 164–68.

22   William B. Hesseltine, *Lincoln and the War Governors* (New York, 1948), p. 108; *New Jersey Senate Journal, 1861* (Belvidere, N.J., 1861), pp. 81, 97–104, 108, 121; Theodore F. Randolph, Trenton, to John J. Crittenden, January 26, 1861, Crittenden MSS; Charles Merriam Knapp, *New Jersey Politics during the Period of the Civil War and Reconstruction* (Geneva, N.Y., 1924), pp. 47–49.

23   Lucius E. Chittenden, *Recollections of President Lincoln and His Administration* (New York, 1891), p. 20; Thurlow Weed, Albany, to Abraham Lincoln, January 28, 1861, R. T. Lincoln Collection; Preston King, Washington, to John Bigelow, February 11, 1861, quoted in John Bigelow, *Retrospections of an Active Life* (5 vols., New York, 1909–13), I, 355.

24   *Detroit Free Press,* February 7, 1861; Walter H. Crockett, *History of Vermont* (New York, 1921), III, 498–99; Chittenden, *Recollections of Lincoln,* p. 19.

25   William A. Buckingham, Norwich, Conn., to R. S. Baldwin, February 4, 1861, Buckingham MSS (photostat in author's possession); *New York Times,* February 4, 1861.

26   Hesseltine, *Lincoln and the War Governors,* p. 107; *New York Times,* February 1, 1861; Washington *Evening Star,* January 31, 1861.

27   Charles Sumner, Washington, to John Andrew, January 23, 1861, Andrew MSS-1; C[harles] S[umner] to John Andrew, "Private," January 26, 1861, *ibid.;* Charles F. Adams, H.R., Washington, to John Andrew, January 28, 1861, *ibid.*

28   John Andrew, Boston, to Charles Sumner, January 30, 1861,

Andrew MSS-2. F. W. Bird, a leading radical legislator, indicated his disapproval of the Governor's reversal in policy. F. W. Bird, Boston, to John Andrew, January 31, 1861, Andrew MSS-1.

29 Charles Sumner to George L. Stearns, telegram, January 31, 1861, Sumner MSS; George L. Stearns, Boston, to Charles Sumner, January 31, 1861, *ibid.;* a digest of the legislative action is carried in the *Boston Advertiser,* January 30, February 1, 2, 5, and 6, 1861.

30 Charles Sumner, Senate Chamber, to John Andrew, "Confidential," January 28 and February 8, 1861; George Morey, Boston, to John Andrew, January 27, 1861, Andrew MSS-2; Amos A. Lawrence, Boston, to Alexander Boteler, February 7, 1861, William C. Rives MSS. The President of the Massachusetts Senate sternly warned Sumner of the political danger inherent in his extremist position: "The truth is there is a desperate effort under, the surface, to drive you from the Senate next winter and if *nothing* is done it is feared by many that the conservative force will get so strong as to drive, both you and Andrew from your seats. . . ."—W. Claflin to Charles Sumner, [January—February, 1861], Sumner MSS.

31 Israel Washburn, Jr., Augusta, Me., to Mrs. W. H. Seward, February 12, 1861, Seward MSS; J. P. Fessenden [written for Uncle by P. B. F.] to W. P. Fessenden, January 10, 1861, Fessenden MSS. Edward Everett described Washburn as "an ultra-Republican."—Everett, MS Diary, Saturday, February 23, 1861.

32 *New York Times,* February 5, 1861; Samuel J. Kirkwood, Executive Office, Iowa, to Hon. James Harlan, James W. Grimes, Samuel R. Curtis, and William Vandever, January 28, 1861, in *Iowa Historical Record* (Iowa City, 1886), II, 375–76; Curtis, MS Journal, February 4, 1861. The Iowa delegation first took the position that "their duties in Congress and to the State" prevented them from serving in the Peace Conference. Later they reversed this position and made occasional appearances.—*Detroit Free Press,* February 7, 1861.

33 *Detroit Free Press,* January 26, 1861.

34 *Delaware House Journal, 1861* (Wilmington, 1861), pp. 335–37, 289; Edward Ridgely, Secretary of Delaware, Dover, Del., to John Letcher, January 30, 1861, Letcher, Executive Papers.

35 *Kentucky House Journal, January, 1861* (Frankfort, 1861), pp. 9, 109–11, 133–40; *Detroit Free Press,* January 18, 1861; Frank H. Heck, "John C. Breckinridge in the Crisis of 1860–1861," *The Journal of Southern History,* XXI (August, 1955), 334.

36 The resolution to send delegates to Montgomery was defeated 11

to 9 in the Senate. A motion to reconsider failed 10 to 10. *Tennessee Senate Journal, January, 1861* (Nashville, 1861), pp. 75–83, 87, 91, 98–107, 111, 115–16, 146–47, 150–51; MS Tennessee Resolutions in Tyler Peace Collection; Lucius E. Chittenden, *A Report of the Debates and Proceedings in the Secret Sessions of the Conference Convention, for Proposing Amendments to the Constitution of the United States Held at Washington, D.C., in February, A.D. 1861* (New York, 1864), pp. 437–38.

37   John W. Ellis, [Raleigh], to Robert N. Gourdin, [December 16, 1860], copy in Ellis, MS Letterbook; John W. Ellis, Raleigh, to I. W. Garrott, January 30, 1861, *ibid.; North Carolina Senate Journal, 1860–1861* (Raleigh, 1861), pp. 209–11, 250; *North Carolina House Journal, 1860–1861* (Raleigh, 1861), pp. 396–97; *Detroit Free Press*, January 29, 1861; J. G. de Roulhac Hamilton, *Reconstruction in North Carolina* (Raleigh, 1906), p. 20.

38   *Missouri House Journal, 1861* (Jefferson City, 1861), pp. 202–6, 218; *Missouri Senate Journal, 1861* (Jefferson City, 1861), pp. 107, 152–53; St. Louis *Missouri Republican*, January 1 and February 1, 1861; *New York Times*, February 9, 1861; Frederick A. Culmer, "A Snapshot of Alexander W. Doniphan, 1808–1887," *Missouri Historical Review*, XXXVIII (October, 1943), 29; Peace Commissioners' Report to the State Convention, in St. Louis *Missouri Republican*, March 6, 1861.

39   J. H. Baker, Office of the Secretary of State, State of Minnesota, St. Paul, to Salmon P. Chase, December 10, 1860, Chase MSS-1.

40   Alexander W. Randall, Madison, Wisc., to Senator J. R. Doolittle, January 17, 1861, Doolittle MSS-2.

41   New Orleans *Picayune*, February 8, 1861, quoted in Dwight L. Dumond (ed.), *Southern Editorials on Secession* (New York, 1931), p. 449.

CHAPTER FIVE

1   Lucius E. Chittenden, *Recollections of President Lincoln and His Administration* (New York, 1891), p. 23; George S. Boutwell, *Reminiscences of Sixty Years in Public Affairs* (2 vols., New York, 1902), I, 268–69; Lucius E. Chittenden, *A Report of the Debates and Proceedings in the Secret Sessions of the Conference Convention, for Proposing Amendments to the Constitution of the United States Held at Washington, D.C., in February, A.D. 1861* (New

York, 1864), pp. 17, 450; Washington *Evening Star,* January 29 and February 9, 1861.

2  Curtis, MS Journal, February 5, 1861; Chittenden, *Report,* pp. 11–13.

3  Washington *Evening Star,* February 6, 1861; Chittenden, *Report,* pp. 12–13.

4  Chittenden, *Report,* pp. 13–14; *New York Times,* February 5, 1861; Chittenden, *Recollections of Lincoln,* p. 23.

5  Lyon G. Tyler, *The Letters and Times of the Tylers* (3 vols., Richmond, 1884–96), II, 625.

6  Quoted from Tyler's announcement in support of Breckinridge and Lane, *New York Semi-Weekly Tribune,* July 13, 1860; Chittenden, *Report,* pp. 14.

7  Chittenden, *Report,* pp. 14–17; Tyler, *Letters,* II, 598.

8  St. Louis *Missouri Republican,* February 9, 1861; Washington *Evening Star,* February 6, 1861; *New York Times,* February 6, 1861.

9  Robert C. Winthrop, Boston, to Tyler, February 12, 1861, Tyler MSS-1; Curtis, MS Journal, February 5, 1861.

10  Chittenden, *Report,* pp. 88, 113, 126.

11  Reuben Hitchcock, Washington, to Peter Hitchcock, Jr., February 10, 1861, Hitchcock MSS.

12  James D. Halyburton, Richmond, to John Tyler, January 25, 1861, Tyler MSS-1.

13  Chase asked that the resolutions be printed for the record.—Chittenden, *Report,* pp. 54, 453–64.

14  *Ibid.,* pp. 64, 77, 169, 414; Curtis, MS Journal, February 3, 1861; John G. Nicolay and John Hay, *Abraham Lincoln: A History* (10 vols., New York, 1904), III, 222.

15  Quoted in the *New York Semi-Weekly Tribune,* February 15, 1861.

16  *Cincinnati Enquirer,* February 13, 1861; Chittenden, *Report,* pp. 68–69.

17  Chittenden, *Report,* pp. 3, 12, 19–21, 27, 29, 32–33, 42–43.

18  Washington *Evening Star,* February 5, 1861; Columbus *Crisis,* February 14, 1861.

19  Chittenden, *Report,* pp. 4, 7, 13, 19, 25, 59, 75. Chittenden also lists ——— Olcott as a secretary, but the contemporary newspaper report is no doubt more accurate. Washington *National Intelligencer,* February 12, 1861. See also J. H. Puleston [New York], to L. E. Chittenden, April 23, n.d., found with [Chittenden], MS Peace Conference Proceedings. Puleston, a British sub-

ject, later was elected to the British Parliament.—James G. Blaine, *Twenty Years in Congress* . . . (2 vols., Norwich, Conn., 1884), I, 269.

20 Printed letter of Crafts J. Wright, Washington, addressed to delegates, March 9, 1861, Corning MSS.

21 Chittenden, *Report,* pp. 23–27, 29, 56. The Tyler speech, for example, was reported, as well as results of the voting.—*Detroit Free Press,* February 9, 1861.

22 J. Z. Goodrich, Washington, to John A. Andrew, February 9 and 10, 1861, Andrew MSS-1.

23 Chittenden, *Report,* pp. 57, 109, 147–48, 158.

24 *Ibid.,* 206–7, 273–75; Alexander W. Doniphan, Washington, to "My dear Jno" [John Doniphan, nephew], February 22, 1861, quoted in Frederick A. Culmer, "A Snapshot of Alexander W. Doniphan, 1808–1887," *Missouri Historical Review,* XXXVIII (October, 1943), 28.

25 Chittenden, *Report,* pp. 21–23; J. H. Puleston, [New York], to L. E. Chittenden, April 23, n.d., found with [Chittenden], MS Peace Conference Proceedings.

26 Chittenden, *Report,* pp. 26–27, 28, 30. Delegates came from Kansas, but Chittenden does not list a representative from that state on the Resolutions Committee.

27 J. Z. Goodrich, Washington, to John A. Andrew, February 12, 1861, Andrew MSS-1.

28 Reverdy Johnson to New York *Journal of Commerce* [n.d.], May 13, 1863, clipping in Tyler MSS-2.

29 J. Z. Goodrich, Washington, to John A. Andrew, February 11, 1861, Andrew MSS-1.

30 Chittenden, *Report,* pp. 28–29, 31–32.

31 J. Z. Goodrich, Washington, to John A. Andrew, February 11, 1861, Andrew MSS-1.

32 Reverdy Johnson to New York *Journal of Commerce* [n.d], May 13, 1863, clipping in Tyler MSS-2; Chittenden, *Report,* pp. 43 ff.

33 John M. Forbes, Washington, to John A. Andrew, February 15, 1861, Andrew MSS-1.

CHAPTER SIX

1 J. Z. Goodrich, Washington, to John A. Andrew, February 7, [1861], Andrew MSS-1.

2 *New York Herald,* December 15, 1860; *New York Semi-Weekly*

*Tribune,* December 4, 1860; Lyman Trumbull to Abraham Lincoln, Washington, December 4, 1860; and E. B. Washburne, Washington, to Lincoln, December 9, 1860, R. T. Lincoln Collection; Kenneth M. Stampp, *And the War Came: The North and the Secession Crisis, 1860–1861* ([Baton Rouge, 1950]), pp. 65, 184.

3  *New York Semi-Weekly Tribune,* December 4, 1860.

4  Carl Schurz, Boston, to J. F. Potter, December 17, 1860, in Frederic Bancroft (ed.), *Speeches, Correspondence and Political Papers of Carl Schurz* (6 vols., New York, 1913), I, 169–70.

5  Horace Greeley, New York, to W. H. Herndon, December 26, 1860, R. T. Lincoln Collection.

6  Thurlow Weed, Albany, to Abraham Lincoln, January 10, 1861, *ibid.* "We have thus far done all in our power to procrastinate, and shall continue to do so, in order to remain in session until after the 4th of March."—Godlove S. Orth to O. P. Morton, Washington, February 21, 1861, Morton MSS.

7  Preston King, Washington, to John Bigelow, February 11, 1861, in John Bigelow, *Retrospections of An Active Life* (5 vols., New York, 1909–13), I, 355.

8  John A. Gilmer, Washington, to Thurlow Weed, January 17, 1861, Weed Collection; Weed, New York, to Abraham Lincoln, February 10, 1861, R. T. Lincoln Collection. "If we can keep Maryland loyal it will not be hard to thrash the rest of niggerdom."—Joseph Medill, Washington, to Charles Henry Ray, "Confidential," January 13, 1861, Henry E. Huntington Library, Ry 85.

9  Frederic Bancroft, *The Life of William Seward* (New York, 1909), II, 21, 36; George S. Boutwell, *Reminiscences of Sixty Years in Public Affairs* (2 vols., New York, 1902), I, 270–71.

10  John W. Ellis, Raleigh, to I. W. Garrott, January 30, 1861, copy in Ellis, MS Letterbook.

11  Daniel M. Barringer, Washington, to John W. Ellis, telegram, February 23, 1861, copy in Ellis, MS Letterbook. A similar attempt was made to influence Tennessee voters. The Nashville *Union* published a telegram from James H. Thomas on election day there: "Conference done nothing yet. Not likely to agree upon anything favorable. No hope of adjustment."—quoted in Nashville *Patriot,* February 12, 1861.

12  S. M. D. Moore, Richmond, to J. D. Davidson, March 10, 1861, Davidson MSS; Judith Page Rives, Castle Hill, [Va.], to ——— [son], January 21, 1861, Alfred Landon Rives MSS; *Richmond Enquirer,* January 14, 1861. John A. Gilmer, Washington, to D. H. Albright, January 8, 1861 [misdated 1860], Gilmer MSS; Alexandria *Virginia Sentinel,* March 7, 1861.

13  Inaugural address, January, 1861, cited in Frederick A. Culmer, "A Snapshot of Alexander W. Doniphan, 1808–1887," *Missouri Historical Review*, XXXVIII, 26.

14  George G. Fogg, Washington, to Gideon Welles, February 5, 1861, Welles MSS-2.

15  See for example O. P. Morton, Indianapolis, to Abraham Lincoln, January 29, 1861; Carl Schurz, Manchester, N.H., to Lincoln, December 18, 1860; David Dudley Field, New York, to Lincoln, January 3, 1861; Elihu B. Washburne, Washington, to Lincoln, January 7, 1861; S. P. Chase, Columbus, to Lincoln, January 28, 1861, R. T. Lincoln Collection. Chase, Columbus, to Charles Sumner, January 26, 1861, Sumner MSS.

16  Joshua R. Giddings, New York, to Grotius [his son], February 5, 1861, Giddings MSS; C. S[umner], Washington, to John A. Andrew, February 10, 1861, Andrew MSS-1.

17  *New York Semi-Weekly Tribune*, February 12 and 15, 1861.

18  Elihu B. Washburne to Abraham Lincoln, January 7, 1861, R. T. Lincoln Collection.

19  *Acts of the General Assembly of the State of Virginia Passed in 1861* (Richmond, 1861), pp. 337–39; Lyon G. Tyler, *The Letters and Times of the Tylers* (3 vols., Richmond, 1884–96), II, 582, 624; John Robertson, Richmond, to John Letcher, February 25, 1861, in *Journal of the Senate of the Commonwealth of Virginia, Extra Session, 1861* (Richmond, 1861), Doc. 25, p. 5.

20  Tyler, *Letters*, II, 588, 590; James Buchanan, Wheatland, to Joseph Holt, March 16, 1861, Holt MSS.

21  John Bassett Moore (ed.), *The Works of James Buchanan, Comprising His Speeches, State Papers, and Private Correspondence* (12 vols., Philadelphia, 1900–11), XI, 118.

22  Tyler, *Letters*, II, 590–91.

23  Certified copy [dated April 5, 1861], J. Holt and I. Toucey, Washington, to James Glynn, W. S. Walker, and other Naval Officers in command, and Adam J. Slemmer, commanding Fort Pickens, January 29, 1861, R. T. Lincoln Collection.

24  Tyler, *Letters*, II, 596; James Buchanan, Washington, to Joseph Holt, January 30, 1861, Holt MSS; John Tyler, Washington, to Buchanan, January 28, 1861, in Moore (ed.), *Works of James Buchanan, XI*, 120–21.

25  Mrs. John Tyler to Mrs. David Gardiner [her mother], February 13, 1861, in Tyler, *Letters,* II, 613; James Buchanan, Washington, to John Tyler, "Private and Confidential," February 21, 1861, Tyler MSS-1; James Buchanan, Washington, to Tyler, February 22, 1861, copy in Holt MSS. Congressman Dan Sickles reportedly

influenced Buchanan to permit the parade. Horatio King, *Turning on the Light* . . . (Philadelphia, 1895), pp. 52–55.

26  Tyler apparently transmitted to Buchanan Governor Pickens' message proposing "to avoid collision and bloodshed."—Tyler, *Letters*, II, 612; *New York Times*, March 4, 1861; Charles Sumner, Washington, to John Andrew, January 28, 1861, Andrew MSS-1.

27  Washington *Evening Star*, February 28, 1861; Mrs. John Tyler to Mrs. David Gardiner, February 3, 1861 in Tyler, *Letters*, II, 596; see also Tyler Peace Collection.

28  John Z. Goodrich, Washington, to John A. Andrew, February 9, 1861, Andrew MSS-1.

29  Henry Greenleaf Pearson, *The Life of John A. Andrew, Governor of Massachusetts, 1861–1865* (2 vols., Boston, 1904), I, 160; Sarah Forbes Hughes (ed.), *Letters and Recollections of John Murray Forbes* (2 vols., Boston, 1900), I, 193–96.

30  Lucius E. Chittenden, *Recollections of President Lincoln and His Administration* (New York, 1891), pp. 37, 58, 64.

31  John E. Wool, Troy, N.Y., to Abraham Lincoln, January 11, 1861, R. T. Lincoln Collection.

32  Francis Fessenden, *Life and Public Services of William Pitt Fessenden* . . . (2 vols., Boston, 1907), I, 120.

33  Senator Grimes spoke once in the Conference when presenting his credentials; Chittenden records no evidence of Senator Harlan's participation, though he was named as a member of the Resolutions Committee.—Lucius E. Chittenden, *A Report of the Debates and Proceedings in the Secret Sessions of the Conference Convention, for Proposing Amendments to the Constitution of the United States Held at Washington, D.C., in February, A.D. 1861* (New York, 1864), p. 17; William Salter, *The Life of James W. Grimes* (New York, 1876), p. 138; Curtis, MS Journal, February 4, 1861.

34  Curtis, MS Journal, January 11, 28, February 21, 1861.

35  James Guthrie, Louisville, to Paul G. Washington, March 13, 1861, Guthrie MSS.

36  J. M. Forbes, [n.p.], to Charles Sumner, February 21, 1861, in J. S. Morrill MSS; A. K. McClure, Harrisburg, to W. P. Fessenden, February 19, 1861, Fessenden MSS.

37  Curtis, MS Journal, January 9, February 22, 23, December 3, 1861; John M. Forbes, Boston, to Zachariah Chandler, January 18, 1861, Chandler MSS.

38  Curtis, MS Journal, December 3, 1861; Curtis, Washington, to Mrs. S. R. Curtis, February 10, 1861, in Kenneth E. Colton, "Ir-

repressible Conflict of 1861: Letters of S. R. Curtis," *Annals of Iowa,* XXIV (1942–43), 30–31.

39   *Detroit Free Press,* February 12, 1861; J. N. Jones, Springfield, Ill., to E. B. Washburne, February 15, 1861, E. B. Washburne MSS; Springfield *Illinois State Journal,* February 20, 1861.

40   Ward & Co., New York, to Thomas Ruffin, February 18, 1861, in J. G. de Roulhac Hamilton (ed.), *The Papers of Thomas Ruffin* (4 vols., Raleigh, N.C., 1918–20), III, 130; Thomas P. Devereux, Connemara, to Ruffin, February 4, 1861, *ibid.,* III, 118.

41   Alexander W. Doniphan to John Doniphan, February 22, 1861, in Culmer, "Doniphan," *Missouri Historical Review,* XXXVIII, 28.

42   Curtis, who wanted his son, Sam, to be postmaster of Denver and Uncle Johnny to be chief clerk in the Register's Office, was "overshadowed and overloaded with applications." Samuel Ryan Curtis, Washington, to Mrs. S. R. Curtis, February 10 and 24, and March 17, 1861, in Colton, "Letters of S. R. Curtis," *Annals of Iowa,* XXIV, 30–31, 34, 38; *New York Times,* March 1, 1861; see Shillington's advertisement, Washington *Evening Star,* February 14, 1861.

43   Amos Tuck, Exeter, N.H., to Richard Yates, December 21, 1860, Yates MSS; Tuck, Exeter, N.H., to Salmon P. Chase, January 14, 1861, Chase MSS-1; John Z. Goodrich, Stockbridge, Mass., to David Davis, November 23, 1860; William Vandever, Washington, to Abraham Lincoln, January 17, 1861; Salmon P. Chase to Lincoln, March 6, 1861, R. T. Lincoln Collection; Charles Buxton Going, *David Wilmot, Free Soiler . . .,* (New York, 1924), pp. 546–47.

44   Godlove S. Orth, LaFayette, Ind., to Schuyler Colfax, November 20, 1860, in J. Herman Schauinger (ed.), "The Letters of Godlove S. Orth," *Indiana Magazine of History,* XL (June, 1944), 160. Valentine B. Horton, for example, had a candidate for First Comptroller of the Treasury.—V. B. Horton, Washington, to Benjamin F. Wade, March 2, 1861, Wade MSS. When the delegation arrived from Kansas, Thomas Ewing, Jr., devoted most of his efforts to getting Governor Charles Robinson appointed Commissioner of Indian Affairs, a post which would assist them both in their railroad promotions.—G. Raymond Gaeddert, *The Birth of Kansas* (Lawrence, Kan., 1940), p. 96.

45   John A. Andrew, Boston, to Charles Sumner, March 11, 1861, Andrew MSS-2; J. Z. Goodrich, Washington, to John A. Andrew, February 25, 1861, Andrew MSS-1.

46   James Pollock, Milton, Pa., to Abraham Lincoln, January 28, 1861;

W. M. McKennan, Washington, Pa., to Lincoln, January 28, 1861; James W. Grimes, Washington, D.C., to Lincoln, January 20, 1961; William Pitt Fessenden, Washington, D.C., to Lincoln, January 20, 1861; Salmon P. Chase, Columbus, to Abraham Lincoln, January 11, 1861, R. T. Lincoln Collection.

47 J. N. Jones, Springfield, Ill., to Elihu B. Washburne, February 13, 1861, E. B. Washburne MSS; B. C. Cook, Washington, to Lyman Trumbull, March 6, 1861; John Wood and B. C. Cook, Washington, to Trumbull, March 6, 1861, Trumbull MSS.

48 Letter of March 17, 1861, quoted in Fessenden, *W. P. Fessenden,* I, 127.

49 Washington *Evening Star,* February 12, 14, and 21, 1861; M. B. Brady to J. M. Tower, [n.d.], Tyler Peace Collection; Chittenden, *Recollections of Lincoln,* p. 41; J. M. Palmer, Washington, to Mrs. John M. Palmer, February 13, 1861, Palmer MSS.

50 Curtis, MS Journal, February 7, 1861; Chittenden, MS Address; Chittenden, *Recollections of Lincoln,* p. 33; Washington *Evening Star,* February 16, 1861; William C. Rives, J. M. Forbes, George B. Rodney, Washington, to Joseph Holt, February 13, 14 and 15, 1861, Holt MSS; A. W. Doniphan, [n.p.], to John Tyler, [n.d.], Tyler Peace Collection; Reverdy Johnson, Washington, to A. W. Bradford, February 26, 1861, Bradford MSS; *New York Times,* February 12, 1861; *New York Semi-Weekly Tribune,* February 19, 1861.

51 John M. Palmer, Washington, to Mrs. J. M. Palmer, February 13, 1861, Palmer MSS; Mrs. John Tyler, Washington, to Mrs. David Gardiner, February 13, 1861, in Tyler, *Letters,* II, 612–13.

52 Washington *Evening Star,* February 14 and 19, 1861; John M. Palmer, Washington, to Mrs. J. M. Palmer, February 13, 1861; John M. Palmer, Washington, to Betty Palmer [his daughter], February 9, 1861, Palmer MSS.

53 *New York Times,* February 5, 8, and 28, 1861; W. N. H. Smith, Washington, to Thomas Ruffin, February 20, 1861, in Hamilton (ed.), *Papers of Thomas Ruffin,* III, 132; *Detroit Free Press,* February 7, 1861.

54 John A. Andrew to Charles Sumner, February 6, 1861, in *Massachusetts Historical Society Proceedings,* LX, 232–33.

55 Chittenden, *Recollections of Lincoln,* pp. 30–31, 35; J. Z. Goodrich, Washington, to John A. Andrew, February 12 and 16, 1861, Andrew MSS-1; *Detroit Free Press,* February 16, 1861; Chittenden, *Recollections of Lincoln,* p. 35.

56 *New York Times,* February 20, 1861; Charleston *Mercury,* February 4, 1861, quoted *ibid.,* February 14, 1861.

57   Mrs. John Tyler, Washington, to Mrs. David Gardiner, February 4, 1861, in Tyler, *Letters,* II, 597.
58   *New York Times,* February 21, 1861. "The prospect of peace gives the politicians of the Cotton States the horrors. What hope have they if precipitation comes to an end; no compromise, no reunion, or they are ruined."—*Louisville Democrat,* February 27, 1861.
59   Alexander Rives to William C. Rives, Jr., February 11, 1861; Alexander Rives to William C. Rives, February 15, 1861, William C. Rives MSS.
60   Chittenden, *Report,* p. 151; Henry T. Shanks, *The Secession Movement in Virginia, 1847–1861* (Richmond, 1934), p.160.
61   *New York Times,* February 12, 13, 16, 18, 19, and 21, 1861; Tyler, *Letters,* II, 613, 616. "Reconstructionists" in the South looked to the rebuilding of the Union on their own terms. "Why, then," observed one Southern editor, "should it not be acknowledged at once ... that the Union is dissolved, *pro tanto,* and that the adhering States should take all steps needful for their own facility in acting, to negotiate fairly upon the grounds of re-union, or the terms for separation?"—New Orleans *Daily Picayune,* February 8, 1861, in Dwight L. Dumond (ed.), *Southern Editorials on Secession* (New York, 1931), p. 449.
62   Chittenden, *Report,* pp. 33–41; Robert G. Gunderson, "John C. Wright and 'the Old Gentlemen's Convention,' " Ohio Historical and Philosophical Society *Bulletin,* XII, 109–18; *New York Times,* February 16, 1861; S. P. Chase, Washington, to William Dennison, telegram, February 13, 1861, Dennison MSS.
63   *Cincinnati Enquirer,* February 14 and 15, 1861.
64   James M. Brown, Massilon, Ohio, to Salmon P. Chase, February 23, 1861, Chase MSS-1.


CHAPTER SEVEN


1   Lucius E. Chittenden, *A Report of the Debates and Proceedings in the Secret Sessions of the Conference Convention, for Proposing Amendments to the Constitution of the United States Held at Washington, D.C., in February, A.D. 1861* (New York, 1864), pp. 534, 45–46; *New York Semi-Weekly Tribune,* February 19, 1861.
2   Reuben Hitchcock, Washington, to Peter Hitchcock, Jr., February [25?], 1861, Hitchcock MSS; "Republican Party Platform, Chi-

cago, Illinois, May 16, 1860," in Henry Steele Commager (ed.), *Documents of American History* (New York, 1934), p. 364.

3 Chittenden, *Report,* p. 70.

4 *Ibid.,* pp. 47–52.

5 *Ibid.,* p. 55; *New York Times,* February 26, 1861.

6 Chittenden, *Report,* p. 320.

7 "A few of the members furnished him with reports of their speeches, but not always in the language used at the time of delivery. My memory of what was said by Mr. Chase and Mr. Frelinghuysen did not correspond with the Chittenden Report."— George S. Boutwell, *Reminiscences of Sixty Years in Public Affairs* (2 vols., New York, 1902), I, 268.

8 Albany *Atlas & Argus,* March 4, 1861.

9 Chittenden, *Report,* pp. 110, 128, 294.

10 *Ibid.,* pp. 116, 128, 294; *New York Semi-Weekly Tribune,* February 22, 1861.

11 Chittenden, *Report,* pp. 89, 316.

12 Nashville, *Patriot,* March 3, 1861.

13 R. S. Baldwin, Norwich, Conn., to W. A. Buckingham, March 4, 1861, in Samuel G. Buckingham, *The Life of William A. Buckingham . . .* (Springfield, Mass., 1894), p. 90.

14 George W. Summers, *Speech on Federal Relations in the Virginia Convention, Delivered March 11, 1861* (Richmond, 1861), p. 4. Political Pamphlets, Virginia State Library.

15 Reuben Hitchcock, Washington, to Peter Hitchcock, Jr., February [25?], 1861, Hitchcock MSS.

16 *New York Semi-Weekly Tribune,* February 15, 1861.

17 J. Z. Goodrich, Washington, to John Andrew, February 16 and 18, 1861, Andrew MSS-1.

18 Chittenden, *Report,* p. 281.

19 A. W. Doniphan, Washington, to John Doniphan, February 22, 1861, in Frederick A. Culmer, "A Snapshot of Alexander W. Doniphan, 1808–1887," *Missouri Historical Review,* XXXVIII (October, 1943), 29.

20 Lucius E. Chittenden, *Recollections of President Lincoln and His Administration* (New York, 1891), pp. 51–52.

21 Chittenden, *Report,* pp. 238, 241.

22 Boutwell called Seddon "the leading man" of the secessionists. —Boutwell, *Reminiscences,* I, 270; Chittenden, *Report,* pp. 96, 320–21.

23 *Ibid.,* pp. 278, 309.

24 *Ibid.,* pp. 94–96.

25 Boutwell, *Reminiscences,* I, 273; Chittenden, *Report,* pp. 99–102.

26   The reporter rather than the speaker is no doubt responsible for the grammar. Chittenden, *Report,* pp. 119, 180, 189, 276.

27   *Ibid.,* pp. 106, 171, 386.

28   *Ibid.,* pp. 119, 126, 152, 154.

29   *Ibid.,* pp. 175, 213–14.

30   *New York Times,* February 18, 19, 20, 21; *Detroit Free Press,* February 22, 1861. James A. Seddon, House of Representatives, to William Wallace, August 23, 1850, Palmer Collection; Chittenden, *Report,* pp. 68, 88, 136, 187.

31   *Ibid.,* pp. 104, 124, 192.

32   *Ibid.,* p. 170; David Dudley Field, New York, to Abraham Lincoln, January 1, 1861, R. T. Lincoln Collection.

33   Chittenden, *Report,* pp. 256, 433.

34   *Ibid.,* pp. 114, 116, 303.

35   *Ibid.,* pp. 306–7, 146–48.

36   *Ibid.,* p. 149; Chittenden, *Recollections of Lincoln,* p. 55.

37   Chittenden, *Report,* pp. 127, 135, 188, 295, 314, 400.

38   *Ibid.,* pp. 172, 214–15, 272, 312, 400–401.


## CHAPTER EIGHT

1   J. Z. Goodrich to John Andrew, February 8 and 11, 1861, Andrew MSS-1.

2   *Detroit Free Press,* February 17, 1861; *New York Times,* February 18, 1861; E. G. Spaulding, House of Representatives, to Thurlow Weed, February 14, 1861, Weed Collection.

3   Zachariah Chandler, Washington, to Austin Blair [handbill "To the Voters of Michigan"], February 11, 1861, Chandler MSS. Contents confirmed in Austin Blair, Lansing, to Chandler, February 27, 1861, *ibid.;* Lucius E. Chittenden, *A Report of the Debates and Proceedings in the Secret Sessions of the Conference Convention, for Proposing Amendments to the Constitution of the United States Held at Washington, D.C., in February, A.D. 1861* (New York, 1864), pp. 468–69; K. S. Bingham, Washington, to Blair, February 15, 1861, *ibid.,* pp. 467–68.

4   *Detroit Free Press,* February 15, 1861; Austin Blair, Lansing, to Michigan House of Representatives, February 14, 1861, in *Michigan House Journal, 1861* (Lansing, 1861), p. 683; John H. Ingersoll, Senate Chamber, Lansing, to Erastus Corning, February 13, 1861, Corning MSS.

5 Ann Arbor *Michigan Argus,* February 8, 15, and 22, 1861.

6 *Detroit Free Press,* February 3, 1861; *Marshall Statesman,* February 6, 1861.

7 Austin Blair, Lansing, to Zachariah Chandler, February 27, 1861, Chandler MSS.

8 *Detroit Free Press,* February 19 and 23, 1861.

9 *Hillsdale County Democrat,* March 13, 1861.

10 Wolverine *Citizen* (Mich.), February 9, 1861, in *New York Semi-Weekly Tribune,* February 22, 1861; correspondence from Leoni, Michigan, [n.d.], *ibid.*

11 *Detroit Free Press,* February 17, 1861. Although the version reported conveyed Bingham's thought, it was not phrased in his language. What he actually wrote was: "... we have been assured by friends upon whom we can rely, that if those two States [Wisconsin and Michigan] should send delegations of true, unflinching men, there would probably be a majority in favor of the Constitution as it is, who would frown down rebellion by the enforcement of laws."—K. S. Bingham, Washington, to Governor Austin Blair, February 15, 1861, in Chittenden, *Report,* Appendix, p. 467.

12 *New York Times,* February 18, 1861; *Detroit Advertiser,* [n.d.], in Madison *Wisconsin State Journal,* February 25, 1861. For accounts of the debates and voting on Virginia's Peace Conference invitation, see *Michigan Senate Journal, 1861* (Lansing, 1861), pp. 197–200, 212, 248 ff., 254, 255, 271, 272, 323, and *Michigan House Journal, 1861,* pp. 544, 683, 690–92.

13 Austin Blair, Lansing, to Zachariah Chandler, February 27, 1861, Chandler MSS.

14 *Detroit Free Press,* January 29, 30, and February 6, 1861; George Warner, Dexter, Mich., to John J. Crittenden, January 24, 1861; extract of letter from R. M. Clelland, Detroit, to Moses Kelly, January 30, 1861, Crittenden MSS.

15 *Detroit Free Press,* February 6, 1861; *Hillsdale County Democrat.* February 13, 1861.

16 Chatfield *Republican* (Minn.), February 13, 1861, quoted in *New York Semi-Weekly Tribune,* February 26, 1861; St. Paul *Minnesotian,* January 16, 1861, quoted in Roman Zorn, "Minnesota Public Opinion and the Secession Controversy, December, 1860—April, 1861," *Mississippi Valley Historical Review* (December, 1949), XXXVI, 445.

17 St. Peter *Tribune* (Minn.), January 30, 1861, *ibid.,* p. 446; Chatfield *Republican,* [n.d.], *ibid.,* p. 455. Charles M. Burt, Red Wing, Minn., to William H. Seward, February 15, 1861, Seward MSS.

18  Zorn, "Minnesota Public Opinion," *Mississippi Valley Historical Review,* XXXVI, 435 fn., 440 fn.; St. Paul *Press,* January 31, 1861, *ibid.,* p. 452.

19  *Minnesota Senate Journal, Third Session* (St. Paul, 1861), pp. 123, 127, 137, 151–52; *Minnesota House Journal, Third Session* (St. Paul, 1861), pp. 165–66.

20  *Minnesota Senate Journal, Third Session,* pp. 149–50, 151–53; *Minnesota House Journal, Third Session,* pp. 166–67, 176–77.

21  Randall quoted in William B. Hesseltine, *Lincoln and the War Governors* (New York, 1948), p. 118; Whitewater *Register* (Wisc.), February 8, 1861; Madison *Argus & Democrat,* February 6 and 8, 1861.

22  D. A. Asham, Milwaukee, to John Letcher, January 25, 1861, Letcher, Executive Papers; Madison *Argus & Democrat,* February 9, 1861.

23  Madison *Argus & Democrat,* February 6, 7, 8 and 9, 1861; *Wisconsin Assembly Journal, 1861* (Madison, 1861), pp. 183–86, 187–89, 191–92, 195, 211, 216, 248–50, 251–54, 260–61, 274, 296–99; *Cincinnati Gazette,* January 30, 1861.

24  Madison *Argus & Democrat,* February 7, 1861; Butler G. Noble, Madison, Wisc. to Thurlow Weed, February 12, 1861, in Thurlow Weed Barnes, *Memoir of Thurlow Weed* (Boston, 1884), p. 317; *Wisconsin Senate Journal, 1861* (Madison, 1861), pp. 115, 123–24, 141–45, 175, 181–83, 192, 195, 220.

25  Madison *Argus & Democrat,* February 9, 1861; *Wisconsin Senate Journal, 1861,* p. 220; *Wisconsin Assembly Journal, 1861,* p. 220.

26  Madison *Argus & Democrat,* February 5 and 14, 1861; Carl Schurz, Springfield, Ill., to J. A. Hadley, February 9, 1861, in Madison *Wisconsin State Journal,* February 13, 1861.

27  Madison *Wisconsin State Journal,* February 13, 1861; Madison *Wisconsin Patriot,* February 14, 1861.

28  Madison *Wisconsin State Journal,* February 20, 1861, Madison *Argus & Democrat,* February 20, 1861. *The Patriot* suggested that Schurz was a part of the conspiracy to "put an end to compromise." "If this be true," said the editor, "it is the most infamous sentiment that an alien Nero could utter...."—Madison *Wisconsin Patriot,* February 23, 1861.

29  Madison *Argus & Democrat,* February 22, 26, and 27, 1861; Madison *Wisconsin Patriot,* February 27, 1861; Madison *Wisconsin State Journal,* February 26 and 28, 1861.

30  Lyman Trumbull to Mark W. Delahay, February 16, 1861, in G. Raymond Gaeddert, *The Birth of Kansas* (Lawrence, Kan., 1940), p. 96; Washington *Evening Star,* February 22, 1861.

31 Document in Tyler Peace Collection.

32 Chittenden, *Report,* pp. 285–88; Washington *Evening Star,* February 22 and 23, 1861; Salmon P. Chase, James S. Wadsworth, and David Dudley Field to Austin Blair, telegram, February 15, 1861, in *Detroit Free Press,* February 17, 1861.

33 *Detroit Free Press,* February 13, 1861; *New York Semi-Weekly Tribune,* February 26, 1861; George S. Boutwell, *Reminiscences of Sixty Years in Public Affairs* (2 vols., New York, 1902), I, 273–74; Chittenden, *Report,* pp. 335, 337.

34 Gaeddert tells the story in all its sordid detail, including a list of beneficiaries from the negotiation of the Delaware and Pottawatomie treaties: Robinson 2,560 acres, Mrs. Robinson 640 acres, Adams 1,280 acres. Ewing, Stone, and a third party received some 26,160 acres, "all at government appraisement." In 1862, Robinson was impeached but acquitted, though "generally supposed to be the biggest rascal in the pile."—Gaeddert, *The Birth of Kansas,* pp. 94–97, 113–14, 187–91.

35 *Ibid.,* p. 96. Why Acting Governor Beebe appointed Robinson's henchmen, and why Governor Robinson appointed rivals from Lane's faction is not clear. Perhaps Robinson's purpose was to keep them occupied elsewhere during the scramble for office.

36 *New York Times,* February 22, 1861.

## CHAPTER NINE

1 Lucius E. Chittenden, *A Report of the Debates and Proceedings in the Secret Sessions of the Conference Convention, for Proposing Amendments to the Constitution of the United States Held at Washington, D.C., in February, A.D. 1861* (New York, 1864), pp. 189, 270 ff.; *New York Times,* February 22, 1861.

2 Chittenden, *Report,* pp. 360, 363–64, 368, 381, 409–10.

3 *Ibid.,* pp. 291, 352. See also Report of Rhode Island Commissioners, *ibid.,* p. 611.

4 *Ibid.,* p. 401. Strong Southern rights advocates used the defeat of this amendment to arouse anti-Union sentiment. Lexington *Kentucky Statesman,* March 1, 1861.

5 Chittenden, *Report,* p. 421; *Cong. Globe,* 36 Cong., 2 sess., 114.

6 Chittenden, *Report,* pp. 307, 334, 407.

7 Alexander W. Doniphan, Washington, to John Doniphan, February 22, 1861, in Frederick A. Culmer, "A Snapshot of Alexander

W. Doniphan, 1808–1887," *Missouri Historical Review,* XXXVIII (October, 1943), 28–29.

8    Nashville *Patriot,* February 15, 1861; *New York Times,* February 14 and 18, 1861; *Louisville Journal,* February 13, 1861; *Cincinnati Enquirer,* February 13, 1861; *Detroit Free Press,* February 20, 1861; Alfred T. Harris, Richmond, to William C. Rives, February 16, 1861, William C. Rives MSS.

9    [Thurlow Weed], Astor House [New York], to William H. Seward, [1861], Seward MSS. For a discussion of the financial pressures for compromise, see Robert G. Gunderson, "Lincoln and Governor Morgan: A Financial Footnote," *The Abraham Lincoln Quarterly,* VI (December, 1951), 431–37.

10   Albany *Atlas & Argus,* February 28 and March 5, 1861. For a full account see Norma B. Cuthbert, *Lincoln and the Baltimore Plot, 1861, From Pinkerton Records and Related Papers* (San Marino, Calif., 1949).

11   [New York] *Express,* [n. d.], reprinted in *New York Semi-Weekly Tribune,* March 1, 1861.

12   *New York Semi-Weekly Tribune,* February 19, 1861.

13   Carlos Martyn, *William E. Dodge, The Christian Merchant* (New York, 1890), pp. 186–87; *Boston Evening Transcript,* February 23, 1861; Washington *Evening Star,* February 23, 1861; Lucius E. Chittenden, *Recollections of President Lincoln and His Administration* (New York, 1891), pp. 68–69; Hiland Hall, Washington, to William H. Seward, February 23, 1861, R. T. Lincoln Collection; *New York Times,* February 27, 1861.

14   Chittenden, *Recollections of Lincoln,* p. 67; Chittenden, *Report,* pp. 336–37; *Detroit Free Press,* February 26, 1861.

15   Washington *Evening Star,* February 25, 1861; *New York Times,* February 25, 1861; Chittenden, *Recollections of Lincoln,* pp. 70–72; Chittenden, MS Address; *Detroit Free Press,* February 26, 1861.

16   Chittenden, *Recollections of Lincoln,* pp. 72 ff.; Chittenden, MS Address.

17   Samuel Bowles, [n.p.], to H. L. Dawes, February 26, 1861, in George S. Merriam, *The Life and Times of Samuel Bowles* (2 vols., New York, 1885), I, 318; Chittenden, MS Address.

18   "Letter written by a prominent member of Congress," Willard's Hotel, Washington, March 1, 1861, in Alexandria *Evening Virginia Sentinel,* March 14, 1861.

19   A. W. Doniphan, Washington, to John Doniphan, February 22, 1861, in Culmer, "Doniphan," *Missouri Historical Review,* XXXVIII, 29.

20 *Louisville Democrat,* February 15, 1861.

21 Chittenden, *Recollections of Lincoln,* pp. 70, 77; Chittenden, MS Address. After a conversation with Lincoln on February 25, J. D. Davidson reported: "I was agreeably disappointed as I had been most unfavorably impressed against him, from the accounts in the papers."—J. D. Davidson, Lexington, Va., to John Letcher, March 2, 1861, Davidson MSS.

22 Chittenden, *Report,* pp. 361, 369; *New York Times,* February 26, 1861; *Detroit Free Press,* February 27, 1861. The *Star* claimed he "was persuaded to remain."—Washington *Evening Star,* February 26, 1861.

23 *Detroit Free Press,* February 27, 1861.

24 Chittenden, *Report,* pp. 330–34, 417, 421, 425, 433; S. P. Chase, Washington, to C. A. Dana, March 1, 1861, Chase MSS-2. *New York Semi-Weekly Tribune,* February 26, 1861. Tyler may have had an important part in drafting Seddon's resolutions. See John Tyler to James Seddon, [n.d.], Tyler Peace Collection.

25 Chittenden, *Report,* p. 90.

26 *Ibid.,* p. 438; Fletcher M. Green, "George Davis, North Carolina Whig and Confederate Statesman, 1820–1896," *The North Carolina Historical Review,* XXIII (October, 1946), 460–61.

27 George S. Boutwell, *Reminiscences of Sixty Years in Public Affairs* (2 vols., New York, 1902), I, 274; Chittenden, *Report,* pp. 438–39.

28 Chittenden, *Report,* p. 439.

29 J. R. Giddings, Jefferson, Ohio, to George W. Julian, February 22, 1861, Giddings-Julian Collection; *New York Times,* February 26, 1861. Greeley was "telegraphed for, on Saturday [February 23], to come on and help to kill off a settlement." "He has grown quite fleshy," the *Star* reported. "His face looks as plump and fat as the body of a picked reed bird in the hight [*sic*] of the shooting season."—Washington *Evening Star,* February 25, 1861.

30 M[ark] H[oward], Washington, to Gideon Welles, [February 25, 1861], Welles MSS-2.

31 W. H. L. Wallace, Washington, to Mrs. Wallace, February 27, 1861, in Harry E. Pratt (ed.), *Concerning Mr. Lincoln . . .* (Springfield, Illinois, 1944), p. 65; *Detroit Free Press,* February 28 and March 2, 1861; Washington *Evening Star,* February 26, 1861; Madison *Wisconsin State Journal,* February 27, 1861.

32 *Detroit Free Press,* February 28, 1861; Charles S. Morehead to John J. Crittenden, February 23, 1862, in Mrs. Chapman Coleman, *The Life of John J. Crittenden . . .* (2 vols., Philadelphia, 1871), II, 338; Liverpool *Mercury* (England), October 13, 1861,

[account of Morehead's speech], in David Rankin Barbee and Milledge L. Bonham, Jr., "Fort Sumter Again," *Mississippi Valley Historical Review,* XXVIII (June, 1941), 71.

33    *Cincinnati Enquirer,* February 14, 1861; *Louisville Journal,* February 16, 1861; Abraham Lincoln, Springfield, Ill., to William H. Seward, "Private and Confidential," February 1, 1861, in Roy P. Basler (ed.), *The Collected Works of Abraham Lincoln* (8 vols. and index, New Brunswick, N.J.), IV, 183.

34    [John M. Palmer], *Personal Recollections of John M. Palmer, the Story of an Earnest Life* (Cincinnati, 1901), p. 84; Thurlow Weed, Washington, to E. D. Morgan, February 28 [1861], Morgan MSS.

35    *New York Semi-Weekly Tribune,* March 5, 1861; John A. King, New York, to the editor, March 1, 1861, in *ibid.,* March 8, 1861. Field's explanation to the New York Legislature is published in Chittenden, *Report,* pp. 596–604.

36    Chittenden, *Report,* p. 441.

37    *Ibid.,* pp. 438, 441–42. Reports of John D. Coalter and Alexander W. Doniphan to the Missouri Convention, in St. Louis *Missouri Republican,* March 6, 1861.

38    Chittenden, *Report,* p. 441; Springfield *Weekly Illinois State Journal,* February 6, 1861.

39    John G. Nicolay and John Hay, *Abraham Lincoln: A History* (10 vols., New York, 1904), III, 232–33; Boutwell, *Reminiscences,* I, 274. St. Louis *Missouri Republican,* February 28, 1861.

40    Thomas Turner, Willard's Hotel, to Abraham Lincoln, February 28, 1861, R. T. Lincoln Collection. Logan may have influenced Palmer who roomed with him in Washington. Senator Trumbull deplored the fact Logan was appointed a commissioner. Lyman Trumbull to W. Jayne, February 17, 1861, Lyman Trumbull Collection; [Palmer], *Recollections,* pp. 88–89.

41    Chittenden, *Report,* pp. 441–45.

42    J. Z. Goodrich, Washington, to John Andrew, February 12, 1861, Andrew MSS-1; C. P. Wolcott to William Dennison, telegram, February 27, 1861, Dennison MSS; *New York Semi-Weekly Tribune,* March 5, 1861. "The Franklin-Guthrie-Crittenden surrender was slipped through the 'one-horse Congress' by nine States to eight, for the want of Mr. Field's vote."—*ibid.,* March 1, 1861.

43    *Chicago Tribune,* [n.d.], quoted in Madison *Wisconsin State Journal,* March 2, 1861.

44    Chittenden, *Report,* pp. 449–52.

45    *Detroit Free Press,* March 1, 1861; *New York Times,* February 28, 1861; Washington *National Intelligencer,* March 2, 1861.

46 Albany *Atlas & Argus,* February 28, 1861; Washington *Evening Star,* February 27, 1861; St. Louis *Missouri Republican,* February 28, 1861.

47 John M. Forbes, Boston, to Charles Sumner, February 28, 1861, Sumner MSS.

## CHAPTER TEN

1 The Tyler quotation is reproduced as recorded. Puleston's letter says 133 delegates participated; actually there were only 132. Lucius E. Chittenden, *A Report of the Debates and Proceedings in the Secret Sessions of the Conference Convention, for Proposing Amendments to the Constitution of the United States Held at Washington, D.C., in February, A.D. 1861* (New York, 1864), p. 452; *Cong. Globe,* 36 Cong., 2 sess., 1254.

2 *Ibid.,* 1262, 1331.

3 *Ibid.,* 1333.

4 *Ibid.,* 1255, 1269–70; Alexandria *Virginia Sentinel,* March 7, 1861. The Crittenden Amendment, said Senator Mason, today "...was postponed on motion of Douglas, to give *precedence* to a joint resolution passed yesterday by the House, proposing as an amendment to the Constitution the *single* article, that no amend.ᵗ should be made to the Constitution, giving power to Congress to abolish *slavery in the states*—To this miserable evasion they have at last come down, to give Virginia and the border states, and Douglas & Crittenden combining, to give it *precedence* in the vote of the Senate, both to the amend.ᵗ of the latter, & that proposed by the peace commissioners—what a commentary on what these gentlemen take to be, the position of our honored state." J. M. Mason, Senate Chamber, Washington, to John Tyler, March 2, 1861, Tyler MSS-1.

5 *Cong. Globe,* 36 Cong., 2 sess., 1310, 1311, 1316, 1344, 1384–85, 1391, 1404, 1405.

6 Chittenden, *Report,* p. 452; *New York Times,* March 1 and 2, 1861; Lyon G. Tyler, *The Letters and Times of the Tylers* (3 vols.. Richmond, 1884–96), II, 616 ff.; Henry T. Shanks, *The Secession Movement in Virginia, 1847–1861* (Richmond, 1934), p. 173.

7 *Richmond Dispatch,* [n.d.], in Alexandria *Virginia Sentinel,* March 7, 1861; *Detroit Free Press,* March 2, 1861; John W. Brockenbrough, Lexington, Va., to Colonel John Rutherford, March 5, 1861, Rutherford MSS.

8  James Guthrie, Louisville, Ky., to Paul G. Washington, March 7, 1861, Guthrie MSS; J. B. Dorman, Richmond, Va., to Cousin James [Davidson], March 31, 1861, Davidson MSS; *Richmond Enquirer,* March 4, 1861.

9  S. M. D. Moore, Richmond, to J. D. Davidson, March 10, 29, and April 6, 1861, Davidson MSS.

10 John Janney, Richmond, to John J. Crittenden, March 12, 1861, Crittenden MSS; William C. Rives, *Speech of Hon. William C. Rives, on the Proceedings of the Peace Conference and the State of the Union, Delivered in Richmond, Va., March 8, 1861* (Richmond, 1861); George W. Summers, *Speech on Federal Relations in the Virginia Convention, Delivered March 11, 1861* (Richmond, 1861); John Letcher, Richmond, to J. D. Davidson, March 17, 1861, Davidson MSS.

11 Tyler, *Letters,* II, 624.

12 J. S. Maxwell, Dallas, N.C., to Z. B. Vance, February 11, 1861, Vance MSS.

13 Wilmington *Daily Journal* (N.C.), March 4, 1861, quoted in Fletcher M. Green, "George Davis, North Carolina Whig and Confederate Statesman, 1820–1896," *The North Carolina Historical Review,* XXIII (October, 1946), 461; David S. Reid, Washington, to Dr. Thomas W. Keen and others, February 18, 1861, Thomas MSS.

14 Bartholomew F. Moore, Raleigh, to Thomas Ruffin, March 7, 1861, in J. G. de Roulhac Hamilton (ed.), *The Papers of Thomas Ruffin* (4 vols., Raleigh, N.C., 1918–20), III, 138–39; John M. Morehead, Greensboro, to Thomas Ruffin, March 5, 1861, *ibid.,* III, 138; John M. Morehead, Greensboro, to D. L. Swain, March 13, 1861, in David L. Swain MSS, University of North Carolina Library. On February 28, North Carolina voters rejected a State Convention by a majority of 651 votes.—J. G. de Roulhac Hamilton, *Reconstruction in North Carolina* (Raleigh, 1906), p. 22.

15 Memphis *Appeal,* [n.d.], quoted in Nashville *Patriot,* March 5, 1861; Memphis *Daily Argus,* February 18, 1861, and Nashville *Union & American,* March 3, 1861, quoted in Mary R. Campbell, "Tennessee and the Union, 1847–1861," *The East Tennessee Historical Society's Publications,* No. 10 (1938), p. 86; Lexington *Kentucky Statesman,* February 26, 1861.

16 *Kentucky Yeoman,* March 20, 1861, quoted in Mary Scrugham, *The Peaceable Americans of 1860–1861, A Study in Public Opinion* (New York, 1921), p. 111 fn.; *Louisville Democrat,* March 3, 1861.

17  Simon Bradford, Memphis, to John J. Crittenden, February 21, 1861, Crittenden MSS; H. P. Bell, agent for the Georgia Secession Convention, testified that the "action of Tennessee would depend largely on the issue of the Washington Conference."—James W. Patton, *Unionism and Reconstruction in Tennessee* (Chapel Hill, 1934), p. 14; Nashville *Patriot,* March 2, 1861.

18  William B. Campbell to A. C. Beard, March 15, 1861, David Campbell MSS, Duke University Library. "For myself I see but two courses for Kentucky to pursue. My first is for a central confederacy. My second is for Kentucky to stand on her own sovereignty. . . ."—Orlando Brown, Frankfort, Ky., to John J. Crittenden, March 7, 1861, Crittenden MSS.

19  St. Louis *Missouri Republican,* March 6 and 17, 1861; Waldo P. Johnson, Oseola, Mo., to Col. John F. Snyder, January 28 and March 11, 1861, Snyder Collection.

20  Reverdy Johnson to New York *Journal of Commerce* [n.d.], May 13, 1863, clipping in Tyler MSS-2. "The obstinate, perverse, demented course of the Black Republicans had had the effect of extinguishing nearly all the conservative feeling which remained in this Commonwealth after the secession of the seven States." Petersburg *Express* (Va.), [n.d.], in Alexandria *Virginia Sentinel,* March 12, 1861.

21  "There is always danger, that when one extreme man of either party changes he becomes more violent on the other extreme." J. D. Davidson, Lexington, Va., to Dear James [Dorman], March 5, 1861, Davidson MSS.

22  Hamilton, *Reconstruction in North Carolina,* p. 19. "The failure of the Peace Conference strengthened the secessionists in Virginia by convincing them that reconciliation was an impossibility."— Shanks, *Secession Movement in Virginia,* p. 172.

23  Rives, *Richmond Speech, March 8, 1861.* A good example of this attitude toward radical Northerners is the comment by a Conditional Unionist leader in the Virginia Convention: "It is idle and wicked for those of us who have already nullified personal and political associations to make further sacrifices in a hopeless cause. If the Public Men at the North hold themselves in their cold repelling position our course is marked and plain. We put Va out of this Union never to return. For one [,] when all my hopes of this Union are surely crushed by Northern men I never wish to be again under a common bond with them[.] Be assured this is the feeling of all the young vigorous controlling Union men here [in the Convention]."—James Barbour, Richmond, to William C. Rives, February 18, 1861, William C. Rives MSS.

24 Thurlow Weed to E. D. Morgan, February 28, 1861, Morgan MSS.

25 Roy P. Basler (ed.), *The Collected Works of Abraham Lincoln* (8 vols. and index, New Brunswick, N.J.), IV, 265.

26 John A. Andrew, Boston, to Abraham Lincoln, March 8, 1861, R. T. Lincoln Collection; E. D. Morgan to Abraham Lincoln, March 5, 1861, *ibid.*

27 Only one Democrat voted against the resolution in the Senate; only five Democrats opposed it in the Assembly.—Madison *Argus & Democrat,* March 7, 1861.

28 *New York Times,* March 5, 1861.

29 *Richmond Enquirer,* March 5, 1861; Lexington *Kentucky Statesman,* March 8, 1861.

30 St. Louis *Missouri Republican,* March 5, 1861. Raleigh *Weekly Register,* March 13, 1861. "The policy indicated towards the seceding States will meet the stern and unyielding resistance of the United South."—Richmond *Whig,* March 5, 1861, quoted in *New York Times,* March 5, 1861.

31 James T. Hale, Washington, to Abraham Lincoln, January 6, 1861, R. T. Lincoln Collection. A number of such appeals also appear in Frederic Bancroft, *The Life of William H. Seward* (New York, 1900), II, 536–42. Seward had told Lincoln that such requests were "very painful."—William H. Seward to Abraham Lincoln, January 27, 1861, R. T. Lincoln Collection.

32 James Guthrie, Louisville, Ky., to Paul G. Washington, March 13, 1861, Guthrie MSS.

33 Orlando Brown, Frankfort, Ky., to John J. Crittenden, March 7, 1861, Crittenden MSS.

34 Chittenden, *Report,* p. 596; Lucius E. Chittenden, *Recollections of President Lincoln and His Administration* (New York, 1891), p. 82; "Treason *should* be coerced."—Springfield *Weekly Illinois State Journal,* December 26, 1860, and March 27, 1861.

35 Chittenden, *Report,* p. 94.

36 Anonymous enclosure "&cc" in letter of H. Lindsly, Nashville, to Lyman Trumbull, January 11, 1861. Trumbull MSS.

37 Abraham Lincoln, Springfield, Ill., to William Kellogg, December 11, 1860, in Basler (ed.), *Collected Works of Abraham Lincoln,* IV, 150.

38 All during February, the *Tribune* ran a column of uncompromising editorials from the various radical newspapers under this heading.—*New York Semi-Weekly Tribune,* April 3, 1861.

*Bibliography*

---

Contemporary newspapers, the legislative journals of participating states, and ninety-three manuscript collections, including the correspondence of eleven governors, have contributed to this account of the genesis of the Peace Conference, of the legislative battles over selection of delegates in the several states, and of the proceedings. Most references are to primary sources, though of course secondary materials have been utilized. Mention of a few such sources risks an injustice to many others, but an indebtedness must be expressed to William E. Baringer, Philip S. Foner, Gilbert G. Glover, David M. Potter, Mary Scrugham, and Kenneth M. Stampp for provocative general works analyzing the events of the immediate pre-Civil War period. Two basic sources by James G. Randall provide excellent bibliographies: *The Civil War and Reconstruction* (rev. ed.; New York, 1953), pp. 881–935, *Lincoln the President* (4 vols., New York, 1945–55), II, 343–400, and with Richard N. Current, IV, 380–98. A Ph.D. dissertation prepared at the University of Florida and available on microfilm from University Microfilms, Ann Arbor, Michigan, gives an evaluation of the proceedings: Jesse Lynn Keene, *The Peace Convention of 1861*, 1955. Of the many state histories consulted, those by G. Raymond Gaeddert, J. G. de Roulhac Hamilton, James W. Patton, Henry T. Shanks, Joseph Carlyle Sitterson, and Kenneth M. Stampp have been particularly useful in clarifying complicated local political situations.

A diligent search has been made for pertinent observations or reminiscences of each of the 132 delegates, sixty-one of whom are described briefly in *The Dictionary of American Biography*. Of all those who left published or unpublished recollections, Lucius E. Chittenden of the Vermont delegation recorded or recalled events with the most realism. Often when the recall of others is hazy, Chittenden provides dramatic detail, recording tears, grimaces, gestures, and epigrammatical phrases. Because of the vividness of his description and for want of other accounts, historians have relied on him for testimony; but, since Chittenden was anything but an impartial witness, he has sometimes subtly projected his prejudices into the works of those who may not sympathize with his point of view. Like Chittenden's three-dimensional memories, those of the mythical "Public Man" tempt the historian because of their highly realistic reconstructions. Both observers successfully create the impression that they personally participated in most of the decisive conversations and events of the secession winter and spring. Because of Chittenden's essential role as unofficial recorder of the Conference, it has been impossible to tell this story without his considerable help. *The Diary of a Public Man,* however, has been rejected as a valid source even for details about dress and weather.

The following MS journals and letters have been of greatest help in describing what took place in the Conference itself: Samuel Ryan Curtis MS Private Journal, John A. Andrew MSS, Reuben Hitchcock MSS, John M. Palmer MSS, William C. Rives MSS, Alfred Landon Rives MSS, and John Tyler MSS. The MS Journals of the Conference, in the handwriting of several individuals, but listed under Lucius E. Chittenden, are separated: February 4 to February 20, New York Public Library; February 16 (*sic*) to February 21, Library of Congress. The published *Official Journal of the Conference Convention . . .* (Washington, 1861) by Crafts J. Wright, Secretary, is available at the Library of Congress. Chittenden's *A Report of the Debates and Proceedings . . .* (New York, 1864) is a more complete digest of the Conference than that hurriedly compiled by the Secretary, but Chittenden made no claim to having furnished "a *verbatim* report."

Efforts to trace materials in the hands of descendants proved to be discouraging. In Tennessee, for example, the Honorable Tom Stewart of Nashville wrote to descendants of each of the twelve delegates; a few promising leads were uncovered, but no useful contemporary accounts of the proceedings. A voluminous correspondence with descendants in other states likewise revealed little evidence.

The letters of the Robert Todd Lincoln Collection disclose far more than John G. Nicolay and John Hay report in their sympathetic ten-volume account. The Lincoln materials at the Illinois State Historical Library and the Henry E. Huntington Library also were helpful. The Thurlow Weed Collection and the William H. Seward MSS at the University of Rochester and the Edwin D. Morgan MSS at the New York State Library are essential to an understanding of the conservative wing of the Republican party. The Erastus Corning MSS at the Albany Institute of History and Art supplement the Weed-Seward correspondence, which together provide a good antidote to the radical accounts frequently quoted from the Elihu B. Washburne MSS, the Lyman Trumbull MSS, the Salmon P. Chase MSS, the Benjamin F. Wade MSS, the Zachariah Chandler MSS, and the Giddings-Julian Correspondence at the Library of Congress.

The following collections are helpful in demonstrating the attitudes of Southern moderates: the William C. Rives MSS, John J. Crittenden MSS, and Alexander A. H. H. Stuart MSS at the Library of Congress; the Alfred Landon Rives MSS, Alexander R. Boteler MSS, and David Campbell MSS at Duke University; the David L. Swain MSS and James Guthrie MSS in the Southern Collection at the University of North Carolina; the Rives Family MSS and the Governor John Letcher Executive MSS at the Virginia State Library; the John A. Gilmer MSS, William A. Graham MSS, and Zebulon B. Vance MSS at the North Carolina State Department of Archives and History; the J. D. Davidson MSS in the McCormick Collection now at the Wisconsin State Historical Society Library; and the T. A. R. Nelson MSS at the Lawson-McGhee Library in Knoxville, Tennessee. Unfortunately, the Guthrie MSS give no information about Conference matters. Apparently Guthrie was too busy as Chairman of the Resolutions Committee to record his reactions to the proceedings; the few available letters concern the operation of the Louisville and Nashville Railroad and are in a scrawl equalled only by that of Horace Greeley.

The John W. Ellis MSS in the Southern Collection at the University of North Carolina are unexcelled for their accounts of the activities of border-state secessionists.

The following manuscripts, newspapers, and periodicals were examined for the period from January to April, 1861:

## Manuscripts

John A. Andrew MSS, Massachusetts Historical Society [MSS-1].
John A. Andrew MSS, Harvard University Library [MSS-2].
Nathaniel P. Banks MSS, Illinois State Historical Library.
Edward Bates MSS, Missouri Historical Society.

Kingsley S. Bingham MSS, Michigan Historical Collections, University of Michigan.

Francis Preston Blair, Jr., MSS, Illinois State Historical Library.

Alexander R. Boteler MSS, Duke University Library.

Alexander R. Boteler Scrapbook I, Duke University Library.

Augustus W. Bradford MSS, Maryland Historical Society (microfilm in author's possession).

Orville H. Browning MSS, Illinois State Historical Library.

William A. Buckingham MSS, Connecticut State Library.

David Campbell MSS, in William Bowen Campbell Collection, Duke University Library.

Zachariah Chandler MSS, Library of Congress.

Salmon P. Chase MSS, Library of Congress [MSS-1].

Salmon P. Chase MSS, Illinois State Historical Library [MSS-2].

Lucius E. Chittenden, MS Account Book, 1845–1873, New York Public Library.

[Lucius E. Chittenden], MS Peace Conference, Washington, D.C., Proceedings, February 4–20, 1861, New York Public Library.

[Lucius E. Chittenden], MS Notes of the Debates in the Conference Convention, February 16, 1860 [*sic* for 1861]—February 21, 1861, Library of Congress.

Lucius E. Chittenden, "President Lincoln and His Administration at the Commencement of the War," MS Address Delivered before the Lyceum at Tarrytown, New York, Friday, March 8, 1867, Henry E. Huntington Library, HM 547.

Thomas J. Clay MSS, Library of Congress.

Erastus Corning MSS, Albany Institute of History and Art.

John J. Crittenden MSS, Library of Congress.

Samuel Ryan Curtis, MS Private Journal, Illinois State Historical Library.

James D. Davidson MSS, McCormick Collection, Wisconsin State Historical Society.

William Dennison MSS, Ohio Historical Society.

Alexander W. Doniphan MSS, Missouri Historical Society.

James R. Doolittle MSS, Library of Congress [MSS-1].

James R. Doolittle MSS, Wisconsin State Historical Society [MSS-2].

Stephen A. Douglas MSS, Illinois State Historical Society.

John W. Ellis MSS, University of North Carolina Library.

John W. Ellis, MS Letterbook, University of North Carolina Library.

Edward Everett, MS Diary, Massachusetts Historical Society.

William Pitt Fessenden MSS, Library of Congress.

William D. Foulke Collection, Indiana State Library.

Giddings-Julian Collection, Library of Congress.
Joshua R. Giddings MSS, Ohio Historical Society.
John A. Gilmer MSS, North Carolina State Department of Archives and History.
William A. Graham MSS, North Carolina State Department of Archives and History.
Horace Greeley MSS, New York Public Library.
James Guthrie MSS, University of North Carolina Library.
Samuel Haycraft MSS, University of Kentucky Library.
Reuben Hitchcock MSS, Western Reserve Historical Society.
Joseph Holt MSS, Library of Congress.
George Washington Jones MSS, University of North Carolina Library.
Ward H. Lamon MSS, Henry E. Huntington Library.
Governor John Letcher, Executive Papers, Virginia State Library.
Abraham Lincoln MSS, Henry E. Huntington Library [MSS-1].
Abraham Lincoln MSS, Illinois State Historical Library [MSS-2].
Robert Todd Lincoln Collection, Library of Congress.
Beriah Magoffin MSS, Kentucky State Historical Society.
George W. Mordecai MSS, Universty of North Carolina Library.
Edwin D. Morgan MSS, New York State Library.
Edwin D. Morgan, MS Letterbook, New York State Library.
Justin S. Morrill MSS, Library of Congress.
Lot M. Morrill MSS, Library of Congress.
Oliver P. Morton MSS, Indiana State Library.
T. A. R. Nelson MSS, McClung Collection, Lawson-McGhee Library.
John M. Palmer MSS, Illinois State Historical Library.
William P. Palmer Collection, Western Reserve Historical Society.
James Pollock MSS, Historical Society of Pennsylvania.
Charles H. Ray MSS, Henry E. Huntington Library.
David Settle Reid MSS, North Carolina State Department of Archives and History.
Rives Family Papers, Virginia State Library.
Alfred Landon Rives MSS, Duke University Library.
William C. Rives MSS, Library of Congress.
John Rutherford MSS, Duke University Library.
Carl Schurz MSS, Wisconsin State Historical Society.
William H. Seward MSS, University of Rochester Library.
John F. Snyder Collection, Missouri Historical Society.
William Sprague MSS, in Mary R. Allen Collection, John Carter Brown Library.
Alexander H. H. Stuart MSS, Library of Congress.
Charles Sumner MSS, Harvard University Library.

David L. Swain MSS, North Carolina State Department of Archives and History [MSS-1].
David L. Swain MSS, University of North Carolina Library [MSS-2].
William H. Thomas MSS, Duke University Library.
Lyman Trumbull Collection, Illinois State Historical Library.
Lyman Trumbull MSS, Library of Congress.
John Tyler, Autograph Signatures of the Peace Convention, Illinois State Historical Library.
John Tyler Peace Convention Collection, 1861, Alderman Library, University of Virginia.
John Tyler MSS, Library of Congress [MSS-1].
John Tyler MSS, Alderman Library, University of Virginia [MSS-2].
John Tyler MSS, Illinois State Historical Library [MSS-3].
Zebulon B. Vance MSS, North Carolina State Department of Archives and History.
Benjamin F. Wade MSS, Library of Congress.
Cadwallader C. Washburn MSS, Wisconsin State Historical Society.
Israel Washburn MSS, Library of Congress.
Elihu B. Washburne MSS, Library of Congress.
Thurlow Weed Collection, University of Rochester Library.
Thurlow Weed MSS, Library of Congress.
Gideon Welles MSS, Henry E. Huntington Library [MSS-1].
Gideon Welles MSS, Illinois State Historical Library [MSS-2].
Gideon Welles, MS Recollections Regarding the Formation of Lincoln's Cabinet, [n.d.], Illinois State Historical Library.
Richard Yates MSS, Illinois State Historical Library.

## Newspapers

Albany *Atlas & Argus.*
Alexandria *Evening Virginia Sentinel.*
Ann Arbor *Michigan Argus.*
*Boston Daily Advertiser.*
*Boston Evening Transcript.*
Boston *Liberator.*
Chillicothe *Scioto Weekly Gazette* (Ohio).
*Cincinnati Commercial.*
*Cincinnati Enquirer.*
*Cincinnati Gazette.*
*Cleveland Plain Dealer.*
Columbus *Crisis.*
*Detroit Free Press.*

*Hillsdale County Democrat* (Michigan).
*Knoxville Weekly Register.*
*Brownlow's Knoxville Whig.*
Lexington *Semi-Weekly Kentucky Statesman.*
*Louisville Democrat.*
*Louisville Journal.*
Madison *Argus & Democrat* (Wisconsin).
Madison *Wisconsin Patriot.*
Madison *Wisconsin State Journal.*
*Marshall Statesman* (Michigan).
*Nashville Patriot.*
*New York Herald.*
*New York Semi-Weekly Tribune.*
*New York Times.*
*Raleigh Weekly Register.*
*Richmond Dispatch.*
*Richmond Enquirer.*
St. Louis *Missouri Republican.*
Springfield *Weekly Illinois State Journal.*
Warrenton *Flag of '98* (Virginia).
Washington *Evening Star.*
Washington *National Intelligencer.*

*Periodicals*

*Harper's Weekly: A Journal of Civilization.*
*Frank Leslie's Illustrated Newspaper.*